ESCAPE

FROM

ABUSE

ESCAPE FROM ABUSE

J. HANNAH LLOYD

COMPANION TO
TIED TO TERROR
SECRETS OF A BATTERED WIFE

This is book two in the *Seasons of Courage* series and also the follow-up to a nonfiction memoir titled *Tied to Terror- Secrets of a Battered Wife*. In the narrative, names and locations are simply products of the author's imagination.

Endorsements

J. Hannah Lloyd's book *Escape from Abuse Survival Guide* is about more than that of a battered wife. Digging deep, layers of trauma, family loss, and health issues are peeled back as she learns to heal from the pain of the past. Guidelines and resources included in this manual provide practical hope for peace and recovery.

—Vonda Skelton
Author, Seeing Through the Lies:
Unmasking the Myths Women Believe

J. Hannah's book, *Escape from Abuse Survival Guide*, details signs and symptoms of abuse and depression so the reader can recognize these in themselves, in a friend, or relative. She also tells the reader what to do in abusive situations, how to get out, and how to heal.

—Pam Zollman
Author, Speaker, Writing Instructor

My heart is on fire after reading J. Hannah Lloyd's exquisitely wrought narrative, *Tied to Terror-Secrets of a Battered Wife*; and now the book *Escape from Abuse Survival Guide*. Battling her way out of the darkness, she emerges with her faith in tact; and walked into a life that was calling her name. And for this we give praise.

—Pamela King Cable
Author of Televenge: the dark side of televangelism

"No weapon formed against you shall prosper, and every tongue which rises against you in judgment you shall condemn" (Isaiah 54:16) (NKJV)

Acknowledgments

To Ann Tatlock, a personal friend and mentor who helped guide me into the world of professional writing. Without her continual support, this book would not have been written. Our friendship is ongoing, and a testimony of how God works out the details of our lives through others. www.anntatlock.com

To Cathy Baker, an award-winning poet and personal friend, who delights in writing, journaling, and blogging. www.cathybaker.org

To Cindy Sproles, who shares a similar background of abuse and survival. She is also an author, writer, and co-founder of the online devotional website: www.ChristianDevotions.us

To my husband of more than twenty-four years, step-father of my children, and a great supporter of my writing craft. His love, sensitivity, and assistance provided ongoing support for the writing of this book, and the first, *Tied to Terror-Secrets of a Battered Wife.*

To Pamela King Cable, a mentor who provided needed guidance that led to the publishing of this book. She is also the author of *Southern Fried Women* and *Televenge—the dark side of televangelism.* www.PamelaKingCable.com

To Pam Zollman, a trusted mentor and children's author, speaker, freelance editor, and writing instructor. www.pamzollman.com and www.thewritersplot.com

To Vonda Skelton, a personal friend and mentor, who teaches the fundamentals of basic writing through critique. She is also the Author of *Seeing through the Lies: Unmasking the Myths Women Believe,* and a coveted Conference speaker. www.VondaSkelton.com

Contents

Chapter One 1
    Battered Wife Syndrome
    What is a Battered Woman?
    Reasons to Leave an Abusive Partner
    Why Women Stay

Chapter Two 9
    Domestic Violence
    Verbal Abuse
    The Abuser
    Physical Abuse
    Events that lead to Violence

Chapter Three 12
    Forms of Abuse
    Emotionally Battered Wife
    Mental Abuse
    Sexual Exploitation and Rape
    Spiritual Abuse
    Shame

Chapter Four 19
    Infidelity
    Signs he may be Cheating
    The Ultimate Betrayal
    Prayer of Unfaithfulness

Chapter Five 23
    Domestic Violence and Children
    Casualties of Divorce
    Violence and Children after Divorce
    Absentee Parent

Chapter Six 29
    Scars of Abuse
    Depression
    Symptoms of Clinical Depression
    Grades of Depression
Chapter Seven 34
    Don't Surrender
    Suicidal Frame of Mind
Chapter Eight 36
    Recovering from Abuse
    Abuse and Disease
Chapter Nine 41
    Understanding Yourself
    Realize you have a Problem
    Examine the Abuse
    Inform Yourself
    Proof he hasn't Changed
Chapter Ten 46
    Help for the Abused
    Prepare for Emergencies
    Have a Plan
    Map your Escape
    Shelters
Chapter Eleven 50
    Phases of Battering
    Characteristics of a Battered Woman
    How Domestic Violence affects Children
    Deliverance
Chapter Twelve 53
    Begin to Heal
    Scars
    Building new Friendships
    Characterization
Chapter Thirteen 58
    Marriage, Abuse, and Divorce
    Deceiver of my Heart
    Healer of my Soul
    God's Grace

Chapter Fourteen 61
 Initiation
 A Father who cares-Devotional
Chapter Fifteen 66
 Roots of Abuse
 Changing the Rules
 A Deserved Thank-You
 Where was He?
Chapter Sixteen 71
 Opposites Attract
 A House that's not a Home
 Forgiveness
 Vengeance
Chapter Seventeen 74
 Generational Abuse
 Like Father—Like Son
 Possessions and Inheritance
 First to Fourth Generations
 Strongholds
Chapter Eighteen 81
 Death of a Marriage
Chapter Nineteen 84
 Bible on Divorce
Chapter Twenty 87
 Certificate of Divorce
 Betrayal
Chapter Twenty-One 89
 When Truth Hurts
 Claws of Abuse
 The Burley Bully
Chapter Twenty-Two 94
 Where Am I?
 Road to Recovery
Chapter Twenty-Three 99
 History of Divorce
Chapter Twenty-Four 101
 More on Battered Wife Syndrome
 From There to Here

Chapter Twenty-Five 105
    Who can I Trust?
    Where is the Love?
    Family History
Chapter Twenty-Six 109
    Rage
    God's Laws vs. Man's Traditions
    A Blind Eye
    Seek Knowledge
    Voice of Wisdom
    Fear God
    Wisdom's Rebuke
Chapter Twenty-Seven 114
    Divine Order
    He who would be Chief
    Family First
    God's Gift is Family
Chapter Twenty-Eight 121
    Family Matters
    How to treat a Wife
    Wrong Choices
    Let the Future Forget the Past
    Steps to Recovery
    A Trace of Sanity
    Acceptance
    Anger and Bitterness
Chapter Twenty-Nine 130
    No Regrets
Chapter Thirty 131
    Forgiveness
    Reasons to Forgive
Chapter Thirty-One 133
    Running From Conflict
    Post Traumatic Stress Disorder
    Intrusive Memories
    Symptoms of Intrusive Memories
    Avoiding the Facts
    Anxiety

Symptoms of Avoidance and Emotional Numbing
Medical Treatment
Panic Attacks
Symptoms of Panic Attacks
Chapter Thirty-Two 144
Role Reversal
Biblical Role of a Husband
Biblical Role of a Wife
Chapter Thirty-Three 146
Medical Battle
Five Steps to Freedom
Good vs. Evil
Never Give up
Chapter Thirty-Four 151
The Police
Can Small Town Police be Trusted?
Georgia on my Mind
Tennessee Recall
Chapter Thirty-Five 155
God is my Helper
Brutal Existence
Why Me?
Chapter Thirty-Six 158
True Wisdom
Prayer of Salvation
Chapter Thirty-Seven 160
Angel
Chapter Thirty-Eight 162
Biblical Encouragement for the Abused
Good for All
New Strength
A Warning against Hypocrisy
The Beatitudes
Chapter Thirty-Nine 169
A New Life
Nothing Hidden
Chapter Forty 172
Moving Forward
Injustices and Forgiveness

Reasons to Forgive
Making Decisions

Conclusion 178

About the Author 188

If things have gone this far, it's time to get help, or get out

Chapter One

Battered Wife Syndrome

What does a woman do when she suddenly realizes she's a victim of domestic violence? And to whom does she turn when no one believes she's being battered?

What is a Battered Woman?

To better understand Battered Wife Syndrome, one should first recognize how a woman becomes battered. Dr. Lenore E. Walker, the nation's most well-known expert on battered women, reports a female must experience at least two complete battering cycles before being labeled a battered woman. Also within this period of time, three obvious phases will occur.

1. Tension-building phase

2. explosion or acute battering incident

3. calm and loving phase—often called the honeymoon stage

Repeated physical and verbal assaults directed at the wife by a husband, or partner, will result in serious physical and psychological damage to the woman. This violence tends to follow a predictable pattern beginning with verbal abuse, and then escalates into dangerous assaults and cruel violence. Most episodes follow an accusation that I call the 'blame game'.

At times, the severity and frequency of assaults may result in death of the female. The longer she remains under the batter's control, the more difficult it will be to make a more permanent escape from her abuser.

More often than not, the woman is blamed for the assault. What remain, following the episode, are emotional and physical scars of abandonment. She will then feel useless, helpless, and hopeless.

Most physical scars heal. But serious emotional baggage often remains to haunt the victim for decades following an assault, or series of assaults.

The battered woman syndrome
n. A pattern of signs and symptoms, such as fear and a perceived inability to escape, appearing in women who are physically and mentally abused over an extended period by a husband or other dominant individual.

¹as·sault

noun
1
a: a violent physical or verbal attack *b*: a concerted effort (as to reach a goal or defeat an adversary)
2
a: a threat or attempt to inflict offensive physical contact or bodily harm on a person (as by lifting a fist in a threatening manner) that puts the person in immediate danger of or in apprehension of such harm or contact—compare battery 1b
b: rape

Synonyms: rape, ravishment, sexual assault, violation

***

Reasons to Leave an Abusive Partner

If your companion displays a combination of the behaviors listed below, you may have a potential batterer on your hands. If so, use caution, or reconsider your commitment.

- **Pushes for quick involvement**: He comes on strong and claims he's never loved anyone like this before. He will then pressure for an exclusive commitment-almost immediately. Over time you will be isolated from all other relationships.

- **Jealous:** He becomes possessive, and calls often to check on you. He will also make unexpected visits, or prevent you from going places you normally go, such as shopping, or even to work, because you "might meet someone else."

- **Controlling:** He excessively interrogates you about who you've talked to and where you've gone. He will also insist that you get his permission before going anywhere, or doing anything.

- **Has strange expectations:** You are expected to be the perfect woman, and meet all his needs and desires.

- **Isolates:** He tries to keep you away from family and friends, and often accuses those close to you of causing problems between the two of you.

- **Condemns:** He blames others for his personal problems and mistakes, and never accepts responsibility for himself. It's always the fault of someone else.

- **Is Hypersensitive:** He complains about things that are just part of everyday life.

- **Cruel to animals and children:** He often kills or irritates animals in sadistic and brutal ways. Sixty-five percent of abusers who beat their partner will also abuse their children.

- **Uses force during sex:** He enjoys throwing you down or holding you against your will during sex. He will also introduce strange methods to make you feel uncomfortable, initiate pain, or require others to participate in the activity with you.

- **Assaults verbally:** He often criticizes, using blatantly cruel or hurtful things while degrading you with cursing and raw language. This is called verbal abuse.

- **Strict and rigid sex roles:** He expects you to obey, and do everything he says without question or hesitation.

- **Mood Swings:** He will switch from sweet and loving to explosively violent behavior. His mood swings are also unpredictable.

- **History of former battering:** He admits to hitting a woman in the past, but blames her for making him do it.

- **Uses threats:** He says "I'll kill you" and then dismisses his threat with "I didn't mean it," or "That's the way everyone talks."

- **Is in Denial:** He tells you no one will ever believe you're being abused. In this way he controls your every move.

Why Women Stay

Often a woman feels tied to a relationship by family pressure, religious dogma, or the desire to raise her children in a complete family unit; which includes both parents. Lack of self-esteem, group support, or inadequate means of financial support will keep a woman under the same roof as her abuser. Her concern in not having enough provision for the children often holds her in a less-than-adequate situation.

As keeper of the peace the woman feels responsible for maintaining the marriage. While in the honeymoon phase of the relationship, she is reinforced, and feels everything in her life is positive. But once she discovers the tenderness was a ruse, she cowers and remains under the man's domination.

Other women stay in a relationship as it feels safer to stay than to leave. Feelings of hopelessness and psychological paralysis will also keep her in dangerous situations. And, because the woman fears for her life, she remains connected to her abuser. His control will make her feel he sees, and knows, her every move. Therefore, she is caught between a desire to leave, and the fear of leaving. In her mind, survival on her own remains a gamble—and perhaps not worth the challenge.

"Hope deferred makes the heart sick, but a longing fulfilled is a tree of life" (Proverbs 13:12)

**The only relative you will ever choose is a spouse.
Seek God's wisdom before you do.**

Chapter Two

Domestic Violence

Although many aspects of abuse have been documented, three are specifically associated with domestic violence.

Verbal Abuse

Abuse is never a justifiable behavior. Seek counsel if you are verbally mistreated. Or, if harsh words hurled at you become a pattern, set boundaries to keep from hearing them. Then create a support system so others are aware of how you feel, and can offer consolation and assistance when needed. Over time, negative words will have negative effects on your self-esteem.

But if verbal abuse has escalated to the physical, perhaps it's time to leave the relationship.

Refuse to engage in verbal or bodily conflict with your abuser. If he becomes angry, try to remain calm, and walk away. Don't let him see a reaction to his words. If you respond, he is being rewarded for his vulgarity and threats. It's also best to disallow him the pleasure of knowing how you really feel.

Leave the marriage, or relationship, if he refuses to seek counsel. Don't allow his words to control your life. But use caution as verbal abuse will most certainly transform into physical abuse. It may also be necessary to break all ties with your abuser, even if that also means his family and friends.

It's also wise to prepare for what may be ahead with information easily available in every corner of your world. The Internet, as a first option, offers multiplied varieties of venues and resources on finding help for domestic violence. Counselors are also easy to locate through a family doctor. Or, find a good attorney who understands domestic violence laws. There's always someone who can help you decide what's best for you, your family, and your situation.

Verbal abuse is easy to hide. However, an abuser in denial will antagonize his wife by using words of shame to degrade her to a lower level. Mocking, cursing, or yelling makes him feel superior, but has far-reaching implications for the abused. Exposure to critical words again and again only causes shame and degradation for the woman.

The Abuser

Below are devices the abuser may use to intimidate his victim.

- Mocks the name she is known by

- Uses vile language to bring her shame

- Yells or threatens to intimidate

- Makes fun of the things she does, the way she fixes her hair, or the clothes she wears

- Manipulates her feelings of self-worth

- Degrades and downplays everything important to her

- Threatens her very life

- Laughs in her face about her friends and family

- Uses swear words to assert his power and bring degradation

- Reminds her of how ugly he thinks she is, and how pretty other women are

- Mocks her when she tries to shield herself from his assaults

- Tells her how utterly deficient she is in the sex department, and how much better other women are

"The tongue has the power of life and death, and those who love it will eat its fruit" (Proverbs 18:21)

Physical Abuse

Physical abuse is easy to identify because the scars are visible, and easy to see. However, when men are violent in a relationship, their one desire is to have complete control over the woman. When he gets physical, he feels strong and domineering. He then allows his anger to rule his emotions. To lead in this way makes him feel important.

But in order to retain his stance he will manipulate the woman with physical force. Being in control makes him feel powerful.

The end result is a woman who is controlled, manipulated, and reduced to a hopeless state of mind.

Physical Abuse Includes:

- Pushing or shoving

- Slapping or hitting

- Beatings

- Punching with a fist

- Biting

- Choking

- Holding the victim down

- Refusing the victim medical treatment

- Throwing items and projectiles at the victim

- Locking the victim outside, in a closet, or separate room

- Threatening the victim

- Trying to make the victim have an accident while driving

- Aggravated battery
-
- Physical or verbal assault

But once the battering is over, the abuser often apologizes. He then expects his victim to forgive, and forget.

"Call to me and I will answer you and tell you great and unsearchable things you do not know. Nevertheless, I will bring health and healing to it; I will heal my people and will let them enjoy abundant peace and security. Give thanks to the LORD Almighty, for the LORD is good; His love endures forever" (Jeremiah 33:2, 6, 11)

Events that Lead to Violence

- Tension builds

- Verbal attacks increase

- A violent outburst occurs

- Abuser blames victim

- Promises to never again batter

- Believes everything is now okay

Over time the woman will retain physical and psychological scars that may never heal. This is a vicious cycle played out again and again on women who don't feel they have a choice in the matter. The damage caused by long term abuse will have emotional, economic, spiritual, and social repercussions; and is a serious concern for society.

Once a beater, always a beater.
Once a batterer, always a batterer.
—Judge Judy Sheilan

Chapter Three

Forms of Abuse

Abuse presents in various forms and degrees. Although some aren't fully understood, all are part of the process of being battered.

Emotionally Battered Woman

- She is isolated from family and friends

- He threatens to take the children away if she doesn't agree with his wishes

- She is accused of being unfaithful, or friends are told she is cheating

- He doesn't want her to be involved with any outside activity such as work, or spending time with friends

- She is criticized about her weight, clothing, or friends

- He expects her to meet his every need without question, and makes her feel guilty if she doesn't comply. If she says no, she is harassed, beaten, or otherwise punished

- He doesn't allow her to make decisions without his approval

- She is degraded so much she feels damaged and useless

Cathy Meyer, a certified divorce coach, marriage educator, and legal investigator reports that emotional abuse in a marriage is such a covert form of domestic violence that many aren't able to recognize themselves as a victim.

A spouse may believe something is wrong. She may also feel stressed out, harbor a sense of depression and anxiety, or be unable to identify the reasoning to clarify those feelings.

Emotional abuse is often used to control, degrade, humiliate, or punish a spouse. Although emotional abuse differs from the physical, the end result is the same.

After many abusive actions, a spouse will become fearful of her partner, and begin to change her behavior just to keep him happy. The more satisfied a partner becomes the less violence the spouse will suffer. But by the time a wife, or partner, identifies her true problem, she feels as if she has gone crazy. She will even doubt her own sense of reality.

Emotional abuse can make her question every thought, and behavior.

Mental Abuse

Mental abuse is an emotional or psychological abuse that may occur in close relationships such as marriage. However, the damage caused by this abuse allows the woman to believe she is worthless, and at fault. It also lowers her self-esteem until she feels useless, and unwanted.

Mental abuse is a consistent and chronic pattern of mistreatment that causes significant distress in the abused. It may also interfere with her ability to develop stable patterns of friendship with others.

The abuser will also intimidate with name calling, blaming, or rejection in order to gain complete control over his victim.

Sexual Exploitation and Rape

Marital rape of a spouse is non-consensual sex where the perpetrator is the victim's husband, or partner. This exploitation is also labeled as domestic violence. In the past it was condoned and ignored by the law. Currently it is considered a criminal assault, and may include divorced or separated ex-spouses, or co-habituating partners. This action is legally equivalent to stranger rape, or date rape. In other countries, however, spousal rape is often accepted as part of the marriage agreement.

Rape is all about anger and control, and not about intimacy. Sex is often used by the male to exploit his aggressive behavior, as he wants to control the victim for various reasons. He could be angry at his mother, or another female, or in retaliation to another abnormal situation. The rapist may even resent women in general, and feel the need to dominate in order to gain his own self-respect.

There are times, however, when a perpetrator will use a child, or woman, for his own sexual gratification. This, however, goes against God and nature, and is an abomination with horrific ramifications.

Victims will carry toxic amounts of shame to the grave unless God is allowed to heal their emotional wounds. While abusers often sift blame from themselves to others, exhibit harsh judgments, and are deceptive in word and deed, victims tend to accept what they have been told as truth. The concept is to believe they deserve what has happened to them.

Being shamed into consent is another ploy used to engage a victim into compliance. However, there is nothing that justifies the sadistic mistreatment of a female. Because the pain inflicted is more than just physical, the emotional aspects of the assault will also be far reaching. Some women will never get over this form of aggression. Even worse is the victimization of a child. The Bible itself speaks against sexual assault.

"...a man...rapes her, only the man who has done this shall die. Do nothing to the woman; she has committed no sin deserving death" (Deuteronomy 22:25, 26)

"He who digs a hole and scoops it out falls into the pit he has made. The trouble he causes recoils on himself; his violence comes down on his own head" (Psalms 7:15, 16)

Breach of the marriage vow with repeated bouts of infidelity is another type of abuse. Mind games that keep one wondering what is true, and what is not, are serious indicators, and will damage a relationship. The inability to trust one's partner is the ultimate violation.

The United States of America has a Declaration of Independence document that declares every citizen has the right to life, liberty, and the pursuit of happiness. But that right can easily be removed by someone who wants complete control over your life. If allowed, they will destroy every ounce of freedom you once had.

How unfair for a woman, married many years to the same man, learn her husband is having an illicit love affair. The marriage then crumbles, and the wife has no choice but to change her lifestyle. Coupled with menopause, grown children leaving the nest, and loneliness, a disaster is waiting to happen. Add a younger woman with flowing hormones to the equation, and enough ammo is available to make any woman go insane. How can anyone justify forcing a faithful wife into such a position?

Only selfish, uncaring, and self-centered men would be so callous, or stoop so low.

Spiritual Abuse

Churches labeled as abusive are characterized as having strong control-oriented leadership. Use of tactics such as guilt, intimidation, and fear often manipulate members while trying to keep them in line. Associates of these churches believe there is no other religious organization that qualifies by belief or standard. They also believe God has singled them out for special purposes higher than traditional churches, and accentuate their stance in order to rebuke others. Dissent is discouraged while subjective experience emphasized.

Member's lives are often subject to scrutiny, rebuke, and embarrassment as rules, legalism, and church dogma abound. Persons and members who rebel are then ceremonially excommunicated.

Using intimidation as a tool, pastors and spiritual leaders often manipulate their position in order to create self-preservation, or for their own gratification. Husbands, as leaders in the home, can also become manipulative toward their wives, and offspring.

Presenting themselves as knowledgeable and qualified, they will use their status to gain access to a victim's sense of dignity, well-being, and self-respect. The stage is then set for the abusive side to move in, and gain access without regard to a victim's sense of purpose. Strict, severe, and spiritual laws have caused some to doubt their own ability to live within the realms of holiness.

Generations of family are raised in a Christian environment. But religion itself keeps members under scrutiny as guidelines are often overbearing, strict, and relentless when one goes astray. Members of these churches are sometimes persecuted by outsiders who don't understand the rules of the church. This may also cause insiders to rebel, and stray from the church altogether.

For example: the basic teachings of Pentecostalism follow the Biblical layout of salvation, but also include the Baptism of the Holy Spirit as relevant to living a spirit-filled life. A downside from my past was a rigid list of rules that restricted members from attending or participating in recreation such as ballgames, dances, or attending movies. The wearing of shorts and swim attire was also strictly prohibited, as were beachgoers, and men who went shirtless.

Women were expected to be chaste in look and deed. Therefore, clothing must depict those beliefs by long below-the-knee dresses, with a disallowance of pants and shorts. Also not allowed was sleeveless clothing as too much of the arm was shown. Make-up and jewelry, including the wedding band, was also prohibited.

The dictates of the church also required that female members grow their hair long, and never visit a beauty shop. The hair requirement for men was short, with accepted length only to the tip of a shirt collar.

Today those beliefs have been dropped as a more modern approach to Christian living has surfaced. But, for some, it's too late as the damage has already been done.

Restraining dominance in religious arenas has caused many to rebel against God, and the church in general. By diminishing one's values, controlling entities place themselves higher in position and knowledge. The victim then remains at risk for a future of misery, heartache, and low self-esteem as their feelings and convictions have been demeaned.

Oppressive rules and regulations have kept many away from church as they've witnessed the domination of stringent supremacy ruin the lives of those entrenched by their methods.

**Big religion may talk the talk,
but do they walk the walk?**

Shame

The implications of this emotion will be strong and are repetitive, leaving powerful feelings of insecurity that come and go. But a victim of abuse often struggles more with these concepts than do others. An inability to overcome your circumstance may become a stronghold in your life. Only God can take away these perceptions, and bring peace to your storm.

- Low self-esteem

- Feeling as if one doesn't belong

- Jealousy

- Insecurity

- Needs to compete with others

- Low-grade depression

- Addicted to a substance, or action

- Wants to blame others

- A tendency to sabotage intimacy in relationships

- An inability to accept criticism

- Hypercritical of self, and others

Allow God to be your strength as you erase the effects of an abusive past.

Chapter Four

Infidelity

A man who maintains a highly respected position in life isn't excuse enough to justify his lust for women. Some will download pornography from the Internet, purchase vulgar and explicit materials, or engage with prostitutes or swinging couples in order to enhance their marriage, or relationship.

"You will have these tassels to look at and so you will remember all the commands of the LORD, that you may obey them and not prostitute yourselves by chasing after the **lust**s of your own hearts and eyes" (Numbers 15:39)

"Do not **lust** in your heart after her beauty or let her captivate you with her eyes" (Proverbs 6:25)

"But I tell you that anyone who looks at a woman **lust**fully has already committed adultery with her in his heart" (Matthew 5:28)

"For everything in the world—the **lust** of the flesh, the **lust** of the eyes, and the pride of life—comes not from the Father but from the world" (1 John 2:16)

Signs He May be Cheating

- He picks fights with you

- He leaves earlier for work, or comes home later than usual

- He acts unappreciated

- He finds fault with everything you do and criticizes you openly

- He becomes distant and uncommunicative

- He changes his behavior when it comes to money issues

- He buys unexpected gifts or does good deeds such as helping clean up

- He changes his style by purchasing different clothing, or loses weight to change his appearance

- He has absences he can't explain

- He tells you there is something wrong with you, and encourages you to get professional help

- He changes his sexual behavior including positions, frequency, or patterns

- There are hang-ups on the phone when you answer his

The Ultimate Betrayal

A cheating man often blames the wife for his adultery. In his mind he is drawing attention away from himself, and believes to have disguised his sin. But, more often then not, the woman has never cheated on her husband, and is appalled when she learns of his unfaithfulness.

In his rants he will use foul language concerning her

alleged infidelity, trying to justify himself. He desires she feel unworthy of him.

But the fact remains, a traitor in the marriage will continue their sinful ways, and most likely, should never again be trusted.

"Not by might nor by power, but by my Spirit,' says the LORD Almighty" (Zechariah 4:6)

I am confident. Fear cannot conquer me.

Prayer of Unfaithfulness

"Have mercy on me, O God, according to your unfailing love; according to your great compassion blot out my transgressions.

Wash away all my iniquity and cleanse me from my sin. For I know my transgressions; and my sin is always before me.

Against you, you only, have I sinned and done what is evil in your sight; so you are right in your verdict and justified when you judge.

Surely I was sinful at birth, sinful from the time my mother conceived me. Yet you desired faithfulness even in the womb; you taught me wisdom in that secret place.

Cleanse me with hyssop, and I will be clean; wash me, and I will be whiter than snow. Let me hear joy and gladness; let the bones you have crushed rejoice. Hide your face from my sins and blot out all my iniquity.

Create in me a pure heart, O God, and renew a steadfast spirit within me. Do not cast me from your presence or take your Holy Spirit from me. Restore to me the joy of your salvation and grant me a willing spirit, to sustain me" (Psalms 51: 1-10)

"Do not be misled: Bad company corrupts good

character" (1 Corinthians 15:33)

"The Lord knows those who are His..." (2 Timothy 2:19)

Emotional wounds will remain as a reminder of outrageous trauma.

Chapter Five

Domestic Violence and Children

When children view domestic violence in the home, they will certainly be affected in negative ways. Research has shown that keeping children with an abuser is not in their best interest. Even when a child sees nothing more than parental violence, but aren't hit themselves, they are affected. Somatic and emotional problems often surface, and are similar to children who have themselves been assaulted. Most will also suffer Post-traumatic Stress Disorder later in life.

A child who learns this type of behavior stays reinforced with a tendency to repeat those same patterns of abuse later in life, as learned at home. But as boys get older, they will identify with the aggressive parent, lose respect for their mother, or feel guilt over their inability to protect her. It's never a good idea for a child to live with an abusive parent. The demonstration of dominance an authoritarian figure shows will also cause a child to become a perpetrator of domestic violence.

Studies found in *The Judges Journal* reveal that spousal abuse typically doesn't stem from relational problems, but instead arises from the man's emotional insecurities, low self-esteem, or a history of abusive behavior as seen in his own childhood.

And since placing a child with an abusive parent long term has proven harmful, if not damaging for a child, it would be wise if the custodial parent be the one who offers the most productive training, love, and attention for the child.

- Placing a child with an abuser perpetuates a cycle of violence by exposing them to an environment where exploitation is acceptable

- A wife-beater's violence damages the emotional health of the couple's children

- The mother normally has better parenting skills because she has, most likely, been the children's primary caregiver

"Now choose life, so that you and your children may live" (Deuteronomy 30:1)

Casualties of Divorce

Children will forever remain the casualties of divorce following their parent's separation. Even if escape from an abusive situation was for their own good, the ramifications may still be devastating.

The financial aspect of the split will also have consequences that are far-reaching. Many times, as a single parent, I had difficulty scraping together enough money to buy just a loaf of bread, or a gallon of milk. Although food was scarce at times, God always came through for us. There were times, however, when all we had were pennies from piggy banks to purchase life-saving sustenance.

But it was during those times of struggle I learned how to trust in God.

"The LORD is my shepherd, I lack nothing" (Psalms 23:1)

"I was young and now I am old, yet I have never

seen the righteous forsaken or their children begging bread" (Psalms 37:25)

"Have I not commanded you? Be strong and courageous. Do not be afraid; do not be discouraged, for the LORD your God will be with you wherever you go" (Joshua 1:9)

Other casualties of divorce are more difficult to swallow. A child's divorce, children searching for identity— even the death of a child isn't unexpected following this type of invasion.

"I waited patiently for the LORD; He turned to me and heard my cry. He lifted me out of the slimy pit, out of the mud and mire; He set my feet on a rock and gave me a firm place to stand. He put a new song in my mouth, a hymn of praise to our God. Many will see and fear and put their trust in the LORD" (Psalms 40: 1-3)

Violence and Children after Divorce

An APA study suggests the after-affects for children following their parent's divorce are relevant to violence in the marriage. Preschool children who became traumatized while observing their mothers being battered also demonstrated negatively in their development.

PTSD and other stress related disorders are also predictable in children when exposed to parental violence again and again; especially when combined with poverty, or their own neglect and mistreatment. Mental illness of one or both parents may also be a risk factor. Even sibling violence is relational to marital violence in the home, and has higher ratings than non-violent homes.

Another study signifies the occurrence rate of childhood abuse in homes where the mother is battered was forty percent. Other results estimate between forty and sixty percent of children raised in violent marriages become easy targets for both parents. Violence in the home is also related to a lack of satisfaction in life which includes low self-esteem and violence among one's own peers, psychological distress, or a lack of closeness with their mother as a young adult.

Children raised in abusive homes are also likely to experience academic and behavioral problems at school. Aggression, delinquency, anti-social behavior, depression, and disobedience toward parents and teachers are not uncommon.

Jeers and insults toward children in an aggressive environment often cause a high-impact child to withdraw into themselves. Buffers to protect the child are good relationships with at least one parent, a sibling, or a friend.

A father's violence will also present in a lack of closeness to their child, or children. Results may vary, but often remain negative, even years after childhood trauma is suffered in the home.

Men need to take their role as husband and father seriously. There are severe consequences to ignoring one's responsibility. How easy it is to destroy the lives of those they love by disregarding their God-given position as head of the household.

In order to raise godly children, one must put God before themselves. Character matters. Lay aside dishonesty, laziness, and lust; and replace with honesty, truth, and reliability. Step up the plate, and be the man you claim to be.

**Which is it? Doesn't know how to give love
or doesn't have love to give?**

Absentee Parent

Just because an absentee parent isn't involved in his child's life doesn't excuse, or make them unaccountable to God, and the child, for a lack of parenting. Many times it's easy to use the excuse of being unavailable because of work, or other activities.

In fact, there's no excuse for a parent to neglect any child brought into this world. Even if their relationship with the other parent doesn't work out, a personal responsibility to nurture and provide for their child is essential, and not excused.

Raising Your Child

Who is raising your child?
Do you want to know who?
Are you really so clueless
That you thought it was you?

What you don't understand
And don't care to see
Is that she's being raised
By her grandpa and me

Who is raising your child?
So you still don't know who?
Well, get a grip on the truth
Because it sure isn't you

©. J. Hannah Lloyd

Kids aren't blind, and understand better than most what's going on in the home. They will also recognize why their parents are divorcing as too many times they've witnessed their mother being assaulted.

Many dads become slack in involvement with their children following a divorce. But in the end, the children will pay a bitter price for his lack of parenting.

I couldn't fix anything, but God could.

Chapter Six

Scars of Abuse

Physical scars usually heal. But the residual of some abuses will linger an entire lifetime.

Depression

Depression is the father of neurosis, or self-hate. This phobia may become overwhelming as one who is possessed with an obsession of loathing, or despondency. But when depressed, one can become lethargic and lose interest in activities, work, or life in general as emotions are sorted through.

Depression often follows a recipient of domestic violence in the home; as dealing with an abuser on a daily basis is confining, and disheartening. It may then become difficult to forgive yourself for various and undefined reasons. Sudden bouts of crying, a serious lack of interest, or withdraw from others can also occur, but is a normal reaction.

Feeling out of control, and unable to change your circumstance will also cause depression.

Many victims suppress emotions too complicated to control. But if conflicts remain overwhelmingly brutal, now is the time to consult a physician—or an attorney.

***

Depression - de·pres·sion

noun \ the size of an angle of depression an act of <u>depressing</u> or a state of being <u>depressed</u>: as *a*: a pressing down : <u>lowering</u> *b (1)*: a state of feeling sad : <u>dejection</u> *(2)*: a psychoneurotic or psychotic disorder marked especially by sadness, inactivity, difficulty in thinking and concentration, a significant increase or decrease in appetite and time spent sleeping, feelings of dejection and hopelessness, and sometimes suicidal tendencies.

Languish

So here I sit
Day after day
As I slowly
Languish away

Sadly afloat
In waves of woe
Wasting away
And feeling low

Don't let me drift
In masked disguise
Please rescue me
Before my demise

©. J. Hannah Lloyd

Depression has been described as living in a black hole while struggling through sensations of sadness, insecurity, and impending dread.

But depression is more than an emotion of sorrow. Feeling listless, hopeless, or abnormal numbness associated with any normal emotion is an instant indicator. Intense feelings of worthlessness, sadness, or anger that interfere with one's ability to eat, sleep, work, or enjoy life in general is another indicator.

There's little relief if overtaken by what is known as clinical depression.

Symptoms of Clinical Depression

- Lack of concentration making it difficult to perform normally

- Feelings of hopelessness and helplessness

- Over-sleeping, or an inability to sleep in a normal way

- Huge consumption of alcohol, drugs, or even food can be another indicator

- Loss of appetite, reckless behavior, or a lack of concern in preserving one's own life

- Presenting as short-tempered, irritable, or more aggressive than normal

- Constant overeating

- Out-of-control negative thoughts and feelings

- Suicidal thoughts

- Unexplained aches and pains

- Self-loathing

- Thoughts of self-injury or manipulation

- Feeling trapped

- An inability to see one's way out of an abusive situation

I Say
(From an abuser's prospective)

I say I can
But then I don't
I say I will
But then I won't

Call me clever
Or call me a fool
Call me incompetent
But I'm going to rule

I say what I say
I am what I am
I do what I do
And it's not a scam

What can I say
To make things right?
What can I do
So we won't fight?

It's not going happen
I'm not going change
I know I am right
And taking no blame

©.J. Hannah Lloyd

Grades of Depression

Categories of depression have separate and unique symptoms, causes, and effects. Understanding what type you have will help the doctor provide the most effective treatment available for your depression.

Listed below are three types of depression a victim of domestic violence may suffer.

- **Atypical Depression** causes weight gain, excessive sleep, an increase in appetite with feelings of heaviness in legs and arms, and rejection sensitivity. If the abuse was short in endurance, this depression should only last a short amount of time.

- **Mild depression** has low-grade symptoms of depression, which may have gone untreated for years. The victim who has suffered domestic violence short in duration over a long period of time may have symptoms not associated with the abuse. However, suppressed feelings of rage caused by the violence will have consequences. Ignoring them will only make it more difficult to understand why feelings of hopelessness surface when least expected.

- **Major Depression** is an inability to enjoy life, or experience pleasure. Seek treatment if this decline lasts longer than six months.

Allowing God to be your guide is the only way to move beyond the pain of abuse

Chapter Seven

Don't Surrender

Although depression varies from person to person, there are common signs and symptoms that indicate a loss of joyfulness. These same symptoms can also be part of life's normal ups and downs. But if the list continues to grow, take note as depression can quickly overtake a person's emotions. Thoughts of suicide may then develop, and could become a major risk factor, or mental disorder.

Despair and hopelessness go hand in hand with domestic violence. These same emotions can also make one believe suicide is the only way to escape the pain of being violated.

Thoughts of death are serious symptoms of depression. Realize that when someone discusses suicide, it's simply a cry for help. Seek assistance if the symptoms listed below are cause for concern.

Suicidal Frame of Mind

- Talks about killing or harming themselves

- Expresses strong emotions about feeling trapped

- Pre-occupation with death

- Acts reckless such as speeding in a car

- Tells people goodbye

- Gives away personal possessions

- Says things like "Nobody loves me," or "I'm useless"

- Mood changes from happy to sad

"...I have set before you life and death...Now choose life..." (Deuteronomy 30:19)

"...hard pressed on every side, but not crushed; perplexed, but not in despair; persecuted, but not abandoned; struck down, but not destroyed" (2 Corinthians 4:8, 9)

Are you capable of surviving beyond an abused, broken, or damaged life? Only God can provide what's needed to overcome depression, and live to tell about it.

Living in the darkness of repression restrains the light of freedom.

Chapter Eight

Recovering From Abuse

Pain and bitterness following a relationship that gone bad, the desire to get even, or a belief that one is worthless describes a woman who's been battered and beaten beyond comprehension by her lover.

To begin the healing process, simply refuse to keep the pain locked inside. Learn to share with others who have also survived similar situations. And realize all emotions left unchecked may become more damaging later in life than when first created. Depression often abounds for those who have escaped an abusive relationship.

Even though the circumstances in one's situation have changed, justification doesn't always provide emotional freedom. It may be time-consuming to work through all the damage caused by an abusive marriage— not only physically, but emotionally. However, your willingness to accept psychological or medical treatment in order to overcome all inflicted injuries may be your salvation.

Depression often surfaces during, and following victimization. The damage may be short lived, or remain for an extended period of time. However, this is normal, and has been documented.

Still, it's best to take responsibility for your own recovery. The refusal of some to believe they really were victimized will only increase in anxiety if not nipped in the bud. But use caution when seeking someone to support your account of the abuse. If they can't be trusted with what you have to say, expecting them to be your advocate is a waste of time.

Also, if one expects justice from the legal system, don't be surprised if expectations fall short. From judges to local police, corrupt policies are in place that often deny protection for those who need it most. The fact remains, you may be on your own, and not yet realize it.

An overwhelming amount of judges side with the assailant, and deny assistance for the victim. One judge recommended a battered woman and her abuser remain under the same roof, but divide the living quarters. A common area would be used for both. The result was a dead wife, beaten to death with a baseball bat in that same area.

Many legal authorities actually assist the perpetrator by withholding needed assistance. The victim is then rendered helpless in the most dangerous of situations.

In today's society it may be necessary to protect yourself. Keep mace or alternative protection close at hand, and preferably on your person. The purchase of a firearm is not an unreasonable option.

At times your actions may be embarrassing for others as you react in unusual ways under duress, and change of routine. Panic and fear following a separation can be non-stop, and quite severe.

Apprehension of what can happen next will cause a victim to cower in expectation of an abusive episode. At this point, it's best to seek medical or psychological assistance in order to completely recover from related feelings of dread caused by a terrorized existence. Information and treatment will provide an immediate benefit, as well as support for years to come. Medication is often helpful in easing the stress caused by a change in lifestyle.

As a casualty of cruelty, you can remain afraid of unplanned encounters with your abuser, even years following your separation. Dread of mistreatment is a continual concern, as it creates noticeable apprehension and nervousness.

Fear can even dictate a victim's very existence. Threats of impending death before and after a separation will keep one scared out of their wits.

Symptoms of a dread disease may later surface when anxiety has hit its limit.

Abuse and Disease

Stress following a sadistic relationship often causes sickness, serious infections, or disease. Also take note that depression is common among people diagnosed with different diseases. However, this does not indicate weak character, and should never be considered shameful enough to remain hidden.

Significant emotional stress often triggers symptoms of sickness. Many studies show the functioning of the immune system to be remarkably altered by emotional stress. Sufferers of a diagnosed disease may have profound emotional consequences as well.

Stress noun \
Definition of: constraining force or influence: as a physical, chemical, or emotional factor that causes bodily or mental tension and may be a factor in disease causation; a state resulting from a stress; *especially*: one of bodily or mental tension resulting from factors that tend to alter an existent equilibrium

Anxiety **anx·i·ety**
noun
plural anx·i·eties

Definition of: a painful or apprehensive uneasiness of mind usually over an impending or anticipated ill b: fearful concern or interest c: a cause of anxiety; an abnormal and overwhelming sense of apprehension and fear often marked by physiological signs (such as sweating, tension, and an increased pulse rate), by doubt concerning the reality and nature of the threat, and by self-doubt concerning one's capacity to cope with it.

Loneliness *lone·ly*

adj \

Definition of: being without company : <u>lone</u> cut off from others: <u>solitary</u> not frequented by human beings: <u>desolate</u> sad from being alone: <u>lonesome</u>

: producing a feeling of bleakness or desolation

— lone·li·ness *noun*

Accusation *ac·cu·sa·tion*

noun \

Definition of

1: the act of <u>accusing</u> : the state or fact of being <u>accused</u>

2: a charge of wrongdoing

Self-Esteem *self–es·teem*

Definition of: *noun*

1: a confidence and satisfaction in oneself: <u>self-respect</u>

2: <u>self-conceit</u>

Depression de·pres·sion ***noun*** \

1: the angular distance of a celestial object below the horizon b: the size of an angle of depression

2: an act of <u>depressing</u> or a state of being <u>depressed</u>

Hope *verb* \

Hoped **hop·ing**

Definition of: intransitive verb

1: to cherish a desire with anticipation <*hopes* for a promotion>

2 *archaic*: <u>trust</u>
transitive verb
1: to desire with expectation of obtainment
2: to expect with confidence : <u>trust</u>
— **hop·er** *noun*
 — **hope against hope** : to hope without any basis for
 expecting fulfillment

 — **Restoration**
 res·to·ra·tion
 Definition of: *noun* \

1: an act of <u>restoring</u> or the condition of being <u>restored</u>: as
a: a bringing back to a former position or condition :
<u>reinstatement</u> <the *restoration* of peace> *b*: <u>restitution</u> *c*: a
restoring to an unimpaired or improved condition <the
restoration of a painting> *d*: the replacing of missing teeth
or crowns
2: something that is restored; *especially*: a representation
or reconstruction of the original form (as of a fossil or a
building)

 "...for thou shalt surely overtake them, and without
fail recover all" (1 Samuel 30:8) (KJV)
 Reach out to others and allow their support to
provide the assistance you need, and desire. Or, find a care
group for abused survivors, and learn from others how to
survive and thrive.
 Sharing information and stories of abuse will be
healing, and therapeutic. New friendships often form that
are encouraging and helpful. And, in this way, you will
understand you're not alone.

Chapter Nine

Understanding Yourself

If one has an inability to understand, perhaps a therapist, or trusted church leader, could be of assistance.

Realize You Have a Problem

Abuse in any form is never acceptable. Advise a friend or relative if you've been mistreated. If they refuse to believe, or provide needed help, find someone who *will* listen, such as the police, or clergy.

If persons around you aren't helpful, keep looking. Unless someone is on your side, it will be difficult, if not impossible, to survive the trauma of abuse.

Keep a journal and record the happenings of violence and abuse after they occur. Journaling will also help to ease feelings of isolation and loneliness, or assist in gaining a better prospective of the situation at hand. If needed, this information can also provide proof of the battering when you speak with an attorney.

Victimization often allows one to remain trapped in an abusive situation for years—even decades. For some it's difficult to understand that battering doesn't occur in normal relationships. Or, perhaps the injured party has never observed a good relationship, and became a victim without realizing the role they played in their own choices.

Examine the Abuse

- It's not your fault. You didn't cause your partner to mistreat you.

- You should be respected, and not battered.

- Everyone, including children, deserve to live in a safe environment, free from the fear of assault

- Don't accept blame for your mistreatment

- You're never alone. There will always be someone who understands, and can provide assistance if asked.

It's often difficult for others to understand why an abused woman doesn't leave the marriage, or relationship. But for the one who's being abused, it's never as simple as just leaving. She has been isolated from her family and personal friends for some time, and is now afraid to stand alone. However, when children are involved, the situation could become more volatile—even dangerous.

Psychologically beaten downs, emotionally drained, financially dependant, and physically threatened on a daily basis makes it difficult for a victim to see a clear way of escape. Feelings of guilt over breaking up the family, or the realization you'll be blamed for what is not your fault, can be overwhelming.

Confusion, desperation, and feelings of entrapment will make one feel it's safer to remain in an abusive household than to strike out on your own. Many will blame themselves. And, because of a weakened emotional status, remain afraid to confront, or seek help.

Understand that your safety, and the well-being of your children, truly does matter. And then decide to never allow the intimidation of others rule your decision to leave an unhealthy, violent, or restrictive relationship.

If they abuse you once, shame on them
If they abuse you twice, shame on you

Inform Yourself

Read about others who have also been abused, and survived. Find resources to provide help with your situation. Or, locate a counseling group of peers who have also survived a similar violence.

Understand that knowledge is power, and appreciate the ability to share with others. There's always comfort in knowing you're not alone.

However, when facing a decision to salvage your abusive relationship, or to leave, keep in mind that your abuser will continue to abuse if you remain. It may be difficult, if not impossible, to reverse those traits because he has a dominant personality. But in order to make an informed decision, research the statistics of domestic abuse relationships; and realize the signs aren't pretty.

Domestic violence has long been a threatening entity with devastating results and irreversible consequences. Abusers often develop deep emotional and psychological problems, sometimes filtering back to their own abused childhood.

Change is never easy, and often unachievable for the abuser. Only his willingness to change delegates his ability to reverse his actions. He must, however, accept full responsibility for his behavior, seek professional treatment, and learn to recognize his role as an abuser. He cannot blame his unhappy childhood, work related circumstances, drug or alcohol habits, or his temper. He alone is solely responsible for the choices he makes in his own life.

It's only natural to want to help your partner. After

all, you did promise to love, honor, and cherish '*till death do us part*. You also believe it's your responsibility to fix his problems because only you can understand everything about him. However, staying in the relationship, and accepting the abuse dumped on you, is only reinforcing the problem, and keeping the action alive.

Remember. It is *not* your responsibility to fix his problems.

Most abusers will make empty promises to stop the battering if threatened with exposure. Later he will plead forgiveness with a guarantee to change. But in this way he continues to control while resuming his verbal and physical assaults. He now believes he's home free as you have never followed through on any one threat to leave the relationship.

But once forgiven, he quickly forgets his promise to stop the abuse as he now realizes you're not going anywhere. However, some abusers will continue their pattern of control, violence, and abusive actions even after the completion of many counseling sessions. Getting help does not guarantee a partner will change.

At this point it may be time to make a more permanent decision. Do you want to continue living in an explosive situation, or is it time to get out?

Also key is to understand just how violence affects children. It's inappropriate to risk your life and their future just to save your marriage. If abuse is rampant, even more essential is the need for safety. Don't allow fear of the unknown to keep you, and the children, in harm's way.

Proof He Hasn't Changed

- If he continues to deny his role as abuser, and minimizes the damage done by his battering

- If he refuses to acknowledge his rage

- If he continues to blame you, or others, for his actions

- If he promises to go to counseling, but doesn't.

- Or, if he refuses attend the sessions unless forced

- If he begs for another chance

- If he tells you he can't change without your help

- If he wants everyone, including children, family, and friends to feel sorry for him

- If he expects something from you in exchange for getting help or treatment

- If he pressures you into making decisions about the relationship, and then blames you when things don't go his way, then he hasn't changed.

Accept the facts and resolve to get help.

Keep your friends close—your enemies even closer

Chapter Ten

Help for the Abused

Until you're ready to leave your abuser, there are things you can do to protect yourself. The safety tips listed below can make the difference between injury or death when trying to escape with your life, and your children.

Prepare for Emergencies

- Be alert to your abuser's red flags. Use caution when he is upset, or shows signs of rage that will result in explosive battering.

- Memorize unbelievable reasons to use as an excuse for leaving the house (day or night) when a violent episode is about to occur.

- Discover safe places in the home to go when your abuser becomes violent, or when an argument becomes volatile.

- Avoid small spaces or enclosed areas without exits such as bathrooms or closets. Only use rooms that have windows or a door in case the need to escape arises.

- If possible, have a portable phone available.

- Use a secret code with your children, friends, or neighbors so they can be alerted if you're in danger, and need police assistance.

Have a Plan

Be prepared to leave the home at any unexpected moment. As a precaution, keep the car full of gas, and parked in a way that makes it easier to get inside and drive away.

- Hide a spare key—just in case.

- Alert the children of your escape plan. But use caution. Children often tell what they know without realizing the consequences.

- Keep a list of trustworthy places to go. Memorize numbers for emergency contacts such as police, shelters, or domestic violence hotlines.

- Use caution so your partner doesn't discover your plan. Cover your tracks. Be careful when using the computer or phone, and don't leave a trail of information behind.

- Use a friend's or public telephone. Most public phones allow a 911 call for free. Or, use a prepaid card so there isn't a trail left to follow.

- Use precaution while using a computer, as with the phone. Change e-mail user names and passwords frequently.

Map Your Escape

Learn what's needed to survive before leaving your abuser. Then hire an attorney to handle the legal applications of obtaining a restraining order, separation agreement, or other legal documentation related to domestic violence issues. Realize you're now the one in control, and allow that motivation to give you the confidence needed to move forward.

Trust only those who understand your pain, and are willing to provide a safe haven for you. Your in-laws and friends may not be the ones to count on at this time.

Don't be afraid to find other advocates if someone you've confided in falls short. There is hope and security somewhere. Keep looking, but remember to use caution when revealing concerns to others. Not everyone can be trusted.

Shelters

Locate a women's shelter in your area if the need for protection becomes essential for survival. However, once you've taken the first step to flee your abuser, it's important to maintain your safety if you plan to survive long-term.

Make sure the information you share is only with people you trust. And use caution, as not everyone who acts responsibly, is. It may also be necessary to move long distances away in order to remain safe. Changing schools for the children may be essential for survival.

Remember to keep all personal information private. Also, be vigilant when sharing phone numbers, addresses, and other important information. Not everyone can be trusted.

Realize that restraining orders may not be enforced if the abuser is known as a good old boy by local police, and others. Some will never believe someone they know is an abuser.

It's also important to stay on guard at all times while fleeing. Until everything has been settled, use every precaution possible for your safety, and the children's.

Or, find a safe place to hide until all conflicts have been resolved in a legal and secure manner.

"I lift up my eyes to the mountains— where does my help come from? My help comes from the LORD, the Maker of heaven and earth" (Psalms 121:1, 2)

With God's help, a leap through a darkened tunnel into the light is achievable.

Chapter Eleven

Phases of Battering

The best way to understand Battered Wife Syndrome is to talk with someone who has survived it. Dr. Lenore E. Walker also writes that a woman will experience at least two battering cycles before she is be labeled a battered woman. This cycle can be broken down into three phases.

The first phase will begin with tension-building moments followed by an explosion of battering episodes. Then a time of calm follows which allows the episode to subside. The third phase includes remorse with petitions of forgiveness from the batterer. Promises to never again repeat the episode will allow a loving relationship to rekindle. This is often referred to as the honeymoon phase.

The abuser's promise to refrain from the beatings will quickly become a lie if the battering is allowed to continue. To ignore the violence only produces future episodes of abuse. And, because women have been programmed to keep the peace in their relationships, they are also inclined to carry the responsibility of holding the marriage together. But this only creates more reasons to stay in the union despite the battering.

Over time the abused will retain low self-esteem, and fear of an inability to provide for themselves and the children. A lack of psychological energy to leave the marriage then surfaces, and the victim again feels helpless to change her situation. Depression follows, and demonstrates as hopelessness at her inability to find someone who understands her situation. This may also trigger self-inflicted obsessions, or suicide.

Battered Wife Syndrome describes a pattern of behavioral and psychological symptoms found in women living in abusive relationships. The dominance their partner creates will, over time, overwhelm as it restricts her ability to think with a clear mind.

Characteristics of a Battered Woman

- She believes the violence is all her fault.

- She's unable to place the responsibility of the battering on anyone else.

- She fears for her life and the lives of her children.

- She believes her abuser knows everything she does, and hears everything she says.

How Domestic Violence Affects Children

Documentation supports the recommendation that, in most states, custody decisions in the courts will not be made without taking domestic violence into consideration. A non-violent parent will also be recommended as there is a presumption against awarding custody of children to an abuser.

Children who witness violence in the home, but aren't hit themselves, demonstrate evidence of emotional and behavioral problems similar to those experienced by children who are physically abused. Children who witness violence will also suffer PTSD at some point in their life. It has also been noted that children who witness aggression from their father may also become sadistic and brutal toward other children. They may even be abusive as an adult.

The older boy often identifies with his aggressive father, and loses respect for his mother; usually because of his inability to provide protection for her when she is assaulted in front of him.

A more consistent predictor of future aggression is children who witness violence between their parents on a regular basis. They have now learned to accept this behavior as normal, and acceptable. Since they see compliance by the victim, they also learn to use those same alternatives in their own relationships. However, this becomes a vicious cycle played out again and again in the lives of many who come from a family where abuse is a normal part of daily living.

It has also been proven that a wife-beater's violence damages the emotional health of his children.

Deliverance

"...hard pressed on every side, but not crushed; perplexed, but not in despair; persecuted, but not abandoned; struck down, but not destroyed" (2 Corinthians 4:8, 9)

The connections in your life will either make you, or break you.

Chapter Twelve

Begin to Heal

Forgive yourself for allowing the abuse to happen in the first place, and continue to pray for the ability to forgive your abuser. Then, as you gain control of your life, release anger and hatred toward your assailant as well as those who protected him, or failed to believe you were in danger. And lastly, be thankful you can now live free from cruelty, manipulation, and the control of a volatile man.

Continue to journal your thoughts and feelings as you move forward into a new lifestyle. Keep a list of resources close at hand for future reference. And, as confidence soars, replace old friends and ex-family with new acquaintances and friends. You're again in charge of your life, and happiness is just around the bend.

Don't become isolated, or withdraw from society. Seek others with whom you can interact, and look for professional guidance if needed. Above all, allow God to be your source of strength and healing. Don't blame him for what others have done to you.

"...forgive one another if any of you has a grievance against someone. Forgive as the LORD forgave you" (Colossians 3:13)

"The LORD is my strength and my defense; He has become my salvation" (Exodus 15:2)

A minister's wife, known for cute phrases and silly clichés was happy to share one with me, a newlywed.

"Where he leads me I will foller," she said. "And when he hits me I will holler."

Although Southern in dialect, her lack of perception or relational experience disallowed knowledge of my situation. But her declaration pierced my heart. Unknown to most, I was living her words.

Scars

Scars from domestic abuse and violence run deep. The trauma you've been through can remain long after you have escaped an abusive situation.

Counseling, therapy, and support groups for domestic abuse survivors will help you process what you've been through as you learn to build new and healthy relationships.

Upsetting scenarios, scary memories, or constant fear of danger ahead may follow the trauma you've just escaped. Numbness, an inability to trust people, or feeling disconnected from the world may also be emotional. Still, in order to embrace a speedy recovery, allow friends and family—the ones you trust—to be your support. The ability to heal and move forward with life is an attainable goal.

Building New Friendships

Use caution when choosing new relationships to replace the old ones. But when searching for intimacy and the support you need, refrain from making quick decisions about your future. Take time, and don't rush into a situation you may later regret. Victims of abuse often repeat their mistakes by selecting relationships that fit the pattern of the assailant they've just separated from.

Decisions concerning romantic relationships should only be made after a complete recovery from all former traumas. A new situation that provides a safe environment for you, and the children, doesn't necessarily mean you're home free.

Continue to seek professional care in order to overcome any abuse-related difficulties that may later develop. But if memories of past abuse continue to surface, the difficulties of coping with them may be more than you can handle.

Substance abuse, alcohol, and eating disorders often become ways of surviving the emotions of cruelty. However, it's best not to allow these crutches to take over your life as more problems will surely develop if allowed. Memories of past abuse have a way of controlling the future, if permitted.

Everyone who experiences mistreatment does so in different ways. Recovery will also be in stages, depending on the type of abuse you've suffered. A victim has little control over the violence imposed. It's important, however, not to accept blame for what you did not initiate.

What *can* be controlled is how you recover your self-respect, and your future. No one deserves to be assaulted, either physically, emotionally, or sexually—whether child or adult.

Remember, you did not cause the abuse. Also understand that your assailant was never your friend.

Those who use the Bible as a weapon to judge, exclude, or condemn is the same as abandoning the Holy Spirit and Jesus as our example.

Once a victim has escaped her abuser, liberation from captivity brings freedom to heart and soul. A prisoner of manipulation and violence has, at last, been released. However, use caution, and restrain from impulsive behavior. Newfound freedom isn't cause for reckless actions as wrong choices will forever affect your future in negative ways.

Independent at last, a comeback into the real world will be exciting and spontaneous; but may also cause irresponsible behavior. Some will act out their freedom in outrageous ways, even going against their own better judgment. For protection, conduct yourself in a safe and responsible way. And realize it will take huge amounts of time to re-adjust, free from the battering that once held you captive.

It's also best not to rush into new love relationships, as the impact of freedom hasn't yet settled in your mind. Don't bond with another man just because you're alone, or believe he will be your salvation.

It may take months, even years, to overcome the damage caused by your assailant. Take baby steps until sound decisions can be made concerning your future.

"...greater is He that is in you, than he that is in the world" (1 John 4:4)

Characterization

"For there is nothing hidden that will not be disclosed, and nothing concealed that will not be known or brought out into the open" (Luke 8:17)

Everyone on the outside believed my marriage was perfect as it appeared that way. However, beneath the façade, our relationship was falling apart. Even support from family and friends wasn't enough to hold the union together. Commitment and integrity were the missing elements.

Jeremy's abusive actions surfaced shortly after our marriage began. And, after a few short years, he wanted out. Destructive actions demonstrated the truth of his spirit. He felt trapped. And, unknown to most, his lustful, roving eye had changed his heart.

Spiteful retaliation then emerged with a vengeance, and assaulted those in the home with hatred. And when his wrath erupted, he became a monster. The aftermath of his rebellion revealed a battered spouse, and three frightened children. But, he did not care.

Biblical knowledge wasn't enough to keep him on the straight and narrow. Even his status as church pastor became irrelevant as he exploited his position. Failing to deter his resolve, family values were then ignored, and carelessly tossed to the wind.

His words and actions indicated a petition for divorce. But his refusal to accept responsibility for that acquisition left me in the lurch.

Yet the truth remained. He wanted me gone. Perhaps if he intensified the battering I would leave. Then everyone would know I was the one who left the marriage, and he would come out smelling like a rose.

And so it was—for a time.

"Then you will know the truth, and the truth will set you free" (John 8:32)

Chapter Thirteen

Marriage, Abuse, and Divorce

"Hope deferred makes the heart sick, but a longing fulfilled is a tree of life" (Proverbs 13:12)

Deceiver of my Heart

According to Cathy Meyer from About.com, a victim of domestic violence should obtain a Restraining Order for protection by the law. Any person who has been subjected to domestic abuse by a spouse, a person who is a present, a former household member, or the victim is eighteen years of age or older, or an emancipated minor, is able to obtain this order.

A victim of any age who has been subjected to domestic violence by a person who she/he says will be the father/mother of the child when the pregnancy is carried to term is also covered under this law. Also included is any person who has been subjected to domestic violence by a person with whom the victim has had a dating relationship.

The occurrence of one or more assaults committed against a victim by an adult or an emancipated minor, is considered domestic violence.

***

Listed below are categories of criminal domestic violence.

- Assault

- Burglary

- Criminal mischief

- Criminal restraint

Healer of my Soul

"May your fountain be blessed, and may you rejoice in the wife of your youth" (Proverbs 5:180)

"You may ask, 'Why?' It's because the LORD is the witness between you and the wife of your youth. You have been unfaithful to her, though she is your partner, the wife of your marriage covenant" (Malachi 2:14)

"Has not the one God made you? You belong to him in body and spirit. And what does the one God seek? Godly offspring. So be on your guard, and do not be unfaithful to the wife of your youth" (Malachi 2:14-16)

Although at times I was venerable, and destitute as a victim of abuse, God knew exactly where I was.

"My dove in the clefts of the rock, in the hiding places on the mountainside, show me your face, let me hear your voice; for your voice is sweet, and your face is lovely" (Song of Solomon 2:14)

"Enduring is your dwelling place, and your nest is set in the rock" (Numbers 24:21) (ESV)

"I will put you in a cleft of the rock, and I will cover you with my hand..." (Exodus 33:2)

"The pride of your heart has deceived you, you who live in the clefts of the rocks..." (Obadiah 1:3)

God Grace

It's not what others have done to us, but what Jesus did for us, that matters. Also key is forgiveness; and essential for healing. With God's help, and the passing of time, the pain of the past can be eliminated. Although some memories remain, peace and tranquility comes with forgiveness.

"...weeping may endure for a night, but joy cometh in the morning" (Psalm 30:5)

The Key

I've lost some needed friendships
Along life's rough highway
Relationships thought endless
Have strangely gone away

I've lost faith in some colleagues
I thought would always care
Like waves and ocean breezes
No longer here, nor there

But with my disappointment
In seasons of great pain
One thing has never wavered
And one thing never changed

I've never lost my praise
And never lost my hope
I've never lost my faith
But cling to heaven's rope

For joy comes in the morning
With love that's pure and free
It conquers pain and hurt
Forgiveness is the key

©. J. Hannah Lloyd

Chapter Fourteen

Initiation

As the recipient of overbearing, restrictive, and reclusive parents, I soon learned that obedience was essential. However, their parenting process was missing an important element—a serious lack of affection. Forced submission was on the agenda but created whelps, blood, and inner turmoil.

Often shunned and ignored as a child, I felt unloved, unwanted, and a burden on family resources. My father was happy only when I worked hard on the farm, stayed out of his way, and restrained from making noise.

On the other side my mother's love presented by inflicting punishment in the form of beatings on a daily basis; most for simple and undeserved infractions. The strength of her arm ruled, as the harshness of her gaze and the tone of her voice intimidated.

Her idea of parenting was *spare the rod and spoil the child*. Although both parents were quick to impose stringent rules, their restrictions made life impossible to enjoy. A distorted perception of relational association created residual indecisiveness that has carried over to the present time.

"Children, obey your parents in the LORD, for this is right" (Ephesians 6:1)

School was also a disappointment as classmates bullied me for my odd name, weather-inappropriate clothing, and restrictive beliefs learned at home and church that I then upheld.

Instigation began with shaming the moment I stepped aboard the school bus as a first grader. Days at school were also tempered with remarks, both demeaning and spiteful. Even following high school, the residual burden of tormentors' evil innuendos continued. A lack of self-esteem, and overt shyness, made it easy to accept bullying as my lot in life.

At the age of fifteen I became a Christian, and life at church began to fill a gigantic void. Boyfriends in the Christian arena then became outlets as I was driven to find the love missing in my home through other venues. A permanent relationship was never the goal.

Restrictions from fornication, however, were essential as my desire for love broke many hearts. When I married at the age of nineteen, I was still a virgin.

However, a chaste lifestyle was never appreciated by my new husband.

Abuse is a secret one doesn't tell. It's just the way life is on any given day.

Both parents ignored the fact that I was being mistreated while married, and refused to support the idea of separation, or divorce. In their eyes, abuse wasn't reason enough to compromise the marriage juncture.

Twelve years later, after the battering accelerated, they relented; and opened their home to me, and my children. But, within one month, we were living in our own place.

There are two sides to a batterer—the polished, public figure that will surface in public settings, and the person who shows up in private.

-Unknown

Family Tree

My grandma gave our family
A lovely orange flowering tree
As many years shaped history
That tree become a legacy

So often Mother would send me
Outside to that family tree
For switches used to thrash my knee
That she would call her whipping tree

Next generation's kids would see
Their grandma sent them on same spree
But I've removed that legacy
For I cut down the family tree

©.J. Hannah Lloyd

My father was a quiet man by nature, but meant exactly what he said; and always obeyed. To my knowledge, he never once struck my mother.

But later, when adulthood was reached, I learned that spousal abuse could exist in a marriage.

A father is to be a concerned supporter of the family. The mother is to be nurturer and protector. However, my parents were neither; and quenched my spirit with overly zealous guidance and limitless restrictions.

"When my father and my mother forsake me, then the LORD will take me up" (Psalms 27:10)

J. HANNAH LLOYD

A Father Who Cares

"Cast all your anxiety on Him because He cares for you" (I Peter 5:7)

On Father's Day the pastor spoke of the importance of having an honorable dad. As he spoke, tears slid down my face, but I quickly brushed them away. Although sensitive to the pain of an un-fulfilled relationship, I was hesitant to acknowledge the hurt. I was afraid.

Often noticed were women happily relating to their fathers as the warmth of his love spilled over their lives like a bubbling waterfall. But, for me, that part of the puzzle was missing.

As a child my mother told me my father didn't want me. And, although I needed him, he didn't need me. But this lack in my life only made love difficult to understand.

Over time I became obsessed in my search for someone to fill that void.

"So, why did I come to church on Father's Day?" I whispered under my breath. "Why am I here?"

I wish there was someone who could make everything right. I need a father.

It was then the Holy Spirit whispered in my ear. "You have a father," he said. "God is your father. And he will make everything right."

A calm, peaceful feeling then settled over my spirit as those words were whispered in my heart. This was going to be a good day after all.

And now, when I'm overwhelmed with the issues of life, and need someone to lean on, I can rest in the arms of my heavenly Father. He's the dad I always wanted, and needed.

**God is faithful and provides in ways
unexplainable to man.**

64

Oh Be Careful Little Eyes

Oh be careful little eyes what you see
Oh be careful little ears what you hear
Oh be careful little hands what you do
For the Father up above
Is looking down in love
So, be careful little hands what you do

Unknown

**Bliss, happiness, elation, and ecstasy—that's all
I really need**

Chapter Fifteen

Roots of Abuse

There is a huge difference between disciplinary spanking and abusive hitting. Exactly when is it appropriate to tell a daughter its okay when you hit her, but not okay for a husband to do the same?

Currently, physical punishment is legal in the United States, although banned in at least twenty-four other countries. And, at least nineteen states allow corporal punishment in their schools.

It's not just a swat on the bottom, study author Tracie Afifi, PhD. University of Manitoba in Winnipeg, reported. It's about physical punishment used regularly to discipline a child. The analysis excluded individuals using more severe maltreatment such as sexual, physical, and emotional abuse as well as neglect; both emotional and physical. It also indicated that parents should be aware of a link between physical punishment and mental disorders in children, reaching into adulthood, and beyond.

According to this same report, researchers examined data from more than 34,000 adults and found that being spanked significantly increased the risk of developing mental health issues as an adult. According to the results, corporal punishment is often associated with mood disorders including depression and anxiety, as well as personality disorders where alcohol and drug abuse are used as a crutch.

In the past, battering in a marriage was ignored. If a girl told her mother the husband was mistreating her, she was cautioned to keep quiet, and not talk about it. The abuse was then swept under the rug, and forgotten by everyone but the one who was battered. And, if exploitation of a minor occurred, this too was denied, and remained a secret.

Violence, foul language, indecent verbal abuse, insults, cruelty, physical and emotional injuries, exploitation, and threats are all part of the equation. If experienced, difficulties of catastrophic proportions will then remain a quandary in the everyday life of a victim.

Even in today's society, violence in the home is a serious concern.

**Every eighteen seconds
a woman is beaten somewhere in the United States
of America**

Changing the Rules

After years of late and sporadic child support, Jeremy, with the help of his new wife, learned to weasel out of paying at all—thus making it difficult for me to support our children on my own. The last presiding judge was also nonchalant, and believed Jeremy's lies of unemployment, albeit he was working, but paid under the table so his wages weren't unaccountable.

His visitation with the children also became infrequent as time moved forward. The first visit following our separation was timely, and expected. Our court-ordered agreement set visitation at every other week-end. But after just a few months he transferred that responsibility to his family, who then took turns driving the distance to pick the children up for visitation. But in the months that followed, this arrangement dropped to once every six weeks until completely non-existent.

Although visits were never refused, neither were they encouraged. Fear for the children's safety was constant; and quite unsettling each time they left for a visit. Horror stories concerning fast driving and irresponsible parenting often followed their return home.

Their last visitation was just before Jeremy remarried. During this visit the children were left with perfect strangers—his future in-laws. After that, they were never again invited for a visit. This was, however, a blessing in disguise.

Soon involved in T-ball, baseball, and soccer, they excelled, and became oblivious to their missing father. Extra-curricular activities through church and school also kept them busy through the week, and on week-ends. Piano lessons, as a focus, required practice; and easily accomplished since trips away no longer remained a quandary.

For the most part Jeremy remained absent from their lives. Soon it was natural to carry on without his influence. But later, as teens, they did need him—mostly for emotional reasons. Yet he remained non-existent. Birthdays and Christmases passed with the regularity of time, but without recognition from him.

"I call on the LORD in my distress, and He answers me. Save me, O LORD, from lying lips and from deceitful tongues. Those who devise wicked schemes are near, but they are far from your law" (Psalms 120:1, 2, 150)

A Deserved Thank-You

It's amazing when one hears a father complain about not being thanked for paying his court-ordered child-support.

A return remark could be, "When have you thanked me, the mother of your children, for everything I've done for them?"

Would he then say?

1. Thank you for teaching my children right from wrong, respect for others, and honesty.
2. Thank you for being the responsible parent twenty-four-seven. I was too busy golfing, playing basketball, or spending time with friends.
3. Thank you for all you've sacrificed so the kids could take expensive field trips, play their favorite instrument in the school band, and wear a name brand pair of shoes like everyone else.
4. Thank you for taking them to the doctor when they were sick, the dentist for care and braces, and church for their spiritual needs. I was too busy with my career, or taking another elaborate vacation, to care.
5. Thank you for staying with my son night and day when he was hospitalized, and for sitting by my daughter's bedside when she was having nightmares.
6. Thank you for soothing the children's broken hearts when I didn't show up for visitation.
7. Thank you for being both mother and father to them—for the shopping, cooking, bill paying, nursing, counseling, the laughter and tears, and the worry over their safety all by yourself.
8. Thank you for soothing their pain when I forgot Christmases, birthdays, graduations, concerts, and everything else because I was too busy to attend.
9. And, most of all, thank you for my children. I look at them with pride, and realize they bare my name, but not my heart.

Compared to the gigantic task of raising a child, how significant is paying child support in a timely manner?

"And when you thank me for all I've done, I'll thank you for making sure your support is paid on time."

Where Was He?

- When his children proudly performed in band concerts at school?

- When they played in various sports while needing approval or assistance?

- When his children graduated from high school?

- When his daughter walked down the isle to be married?

- When important events involving the children came and went without even a phone call to cheer them on?

- When his youngest needed affirmation and direction as a teen?

- When the children needed a firm hand, or a kind shoulder to lean on?

- Where was he?

"A good man brings good things out of the good stored up in him, and an evil man brings evil things out of the evil stored up in him" (Matthew 12:35)

If you bungle raising your children, I don't think whatever else you do well matters very much.

Jacqueline Kennedy Onassis

Chapter Sixteen

Opposites Attract

When a couple first meet, their attraction may be instantaneous. However, romantically involved too fast often evolves into disappointment, and regret. The couple may truly be incompatible due to dissimilar backgrounds, different goals, and opposite desires.

An opposite may be the one to look for when searching for a short, passionate relationship. But most will look for someone comparable to themselves, instead of someone totally opposite. Yet, finding someone for a long-term relationship, or someone to marry, takes time, and understanding.

Learn more about yourself so you are able to choose a companion who is truly compatible.

A House that's Not a Home

"...Has anyone built a new **house** and **not** dedicated it? Let him go **home**, or he may die in battle and someone else may dedicate it" (Deuteronomy 20:5)

When is a house not a home?

Where un-forgiveness abounds, or restrictions overwhelm—when dictatorship rules, or impatience complains. Where children are ignored, abused, or hated. And when a man's true love isn't his wife, but himself.

"If a house is divided against itself, that house

cannot stand" (Mark 3:25)

Forgiveness

"Why should I be the one to forgive? I didn't ask to be abused. He should be the one to ask me for forgiveness. After all, I'm the one who's hurting, not him. Besides, he doesn't deserve my forgiveness."

Forgiving your abuser doesn't excuse what's been done to you. It doesn't matter if the relationship was long lasting, or short lived—desired, or despised. It only signifies that, in order to move on with your life, it's essential to absolve your abuser. Forgiveness is crucial to overcoming the hurdle of mistreatment. However, this does not mean we forget, or agree to continue accepting the abuse.

Forgiveness is free. Trust must be earned.

Withdrawing from society is pointless. It's best to confront your reality, and choose to forgive so the past doesn't dominate the future. When forgiveness is relinquished, freedom is paid for.

Reconciliation isn't required in order to forgive. It only means the abuser no longer has control over your life.

Vengeance

"Bless those who persecute you; bless and do not curse. Rejoice with those who rejoice; mourn with those who mourn. Live in harmony with one another. Do not be proud, but willing to associate with people of low position. Do not be conceited.

Do not repay anyone evil for evil. Be careful to do what is right in the eyes of everyone. If it's possible, as far as it depends on you, live at peace with everyone. Do not take revenge, my dear friends, but leave room for God's wrath, for it is written: "It is mine to avenge; I will repay, says the Lord." On the contrary: "If your enemy is hungry, feed him; if he is thirsty, give him something to drink. In doing this, you will heap burning coals on his head. Do not be overcome by evil, but overcome evil with good" (Romans 12:14-21)

"A good man brings good things out of the good stored up in his heart, and an evil man brings evil things out of the evil stored up in his heart. For the mouth speaks what the heart is full of" (Luke 6:45)

Chapter Seventeen

Generational Abuse

Throughout childhood, cycles of abuse may play out on playmates, family members, and friends. Uncontrollable behavior has, most likely, been learned at home, but kept hidden. However, what a child sees when small remains a leaned behavior as an adult. If abuse is observed as an adolescent, the battering of others is not unexpected.

Parental secrets are often exposed after the child becomes older, and repeats behavior learned while in the home. Battering may then become a natural occurrence if not blocked by interceptive measures. Psychological treatment may also be needed to control a desire to violate.

Cycles of generational abuse are passed down by example and exposure—from parent to child. Episodic abuse occurs in a pattern of repetition within the context of at least two individuals within a family system. It may also involve child abuse, spousal abuse, or even elder abuse.

A son who is verbally or physically abused by his father will, most likely, mistreat his own children in the same way. A daughter who hears her mother tear down, criticize, or belittle the father will also adapt to this same behavior; which involves verbal control. A child who sees parents engage in abusive behavior toward each other will often violate his or her own spouse in similar ways. These are all examples of generational abuse.

Most families have a member they secretly call the Black Sheep. Although most in the family accept them as one of their own, many cringe when they do. Most Black

Sheep are also shunned by outsiders due to the embarrassment they tend to cause.

Odd family members are rebels by nature, or respond in eccentric ways society doesn't accept, as a general rule. The strange way they dress, or weird habits they portray, are often cause for rejection. The title of Black Sheep is also bestowed because one member comes across as too bold, or not conspicuous enough; therefore making them abnormal by definition.

But for others, a Black Sheep may be the one who goes against family tradition by disregarding the unit's reputation, customs, or convictions; therefore rendering themselves an outcast in their own lineage.

Like Father—Like Son

Jeremy's father was a prime example of the Black Sheep anomaly. Although generations in his family were Christian, he himself denounced church teachings and Biblical truth for another woman. During his rebellion, he divorced his first wife, and married another; leaving four children fatherless in the home.

Informing family, friends, and an entire church congregation his first wife had committed adultery was lie number one. He then portrayed himself as the model of marriage and family; even later serving in respectable church positions.

His second marriage was based on lies, deceit, and hypocrisy. A lack of integrity was apparent as the children from his first marriage grew up without a father's love and attention.

The first wife did not believe in divorce. After their break-up she never re-married, but considered herself a widowed woman until her death.

In the aftermath, both daughters chose their own bitter paths to take. The first conceived a child out of wedlock. The second, while married, conceived a child with another man whom she later married after divorcing the first husband.

His sons also had demons to chase. Jeremy, the oldest, and my first husband, had affairs on the side, and was brutal and abusive toward me—his first wife. He also chose to be non-existent concerning his own children following our divorce. He was named for his father, and was, without a doubt, his father's son.

Another son, although married, has never fathered children.

The last child, conceived with the second wife, is the *only* child by action and deed.

"...For I the LORD your God am a jealous God, visiting the iniquity of the fathers upon the children unto the third and fourth generation of them that hate me" (Exodus 20:5)

Devastation following this family is now in the fourth generation. If one retraces their own family line, God's truth will speak volumes concerning generations of family in relation to Exodus 20:5. Many families have similar backgrounds, but few are willing to talk about them.

The offspring from my father-in-law's first marriage also suffered further humiliation at his funeral. Not only were they excluded from participating in the interment, or eulogies, but none were invited to speak on behalf of their siblings. Instead, an outside member was the appointed spokesman.

The funeral itself must certainly have been offensive to the first offspring as the deceased was described as a wonderful, loving man. But they never experienced that love as children, and remain devastated their father chose a woman over them.

The ceremony itself was traditional military, with all

the required pomp and circumstance. The committal, however, was less than soothing as the original family were somewhat shunned by their father's friends, and members of his church.

In the past, the first wife recalled many difficulties while raising four children without a husband. Not only was she shunned as a divorcée, but also blamed for lies she had no control over.

And, because Jeremy followed in his father's footsteps, I was also a recipient of the father's sin.

Jeremy died at the age of forty-three after suffering three separate cancers following our divorce. The first was breast cancer, for which he was treated, and declared cancer free. The disease then migrated to his leg bones. After treatment he was again declared cancer free. But the cancer resurfaced—this time in the brain.

Surgery allowed a short respite before his death. His second wife and her child, however, were the only recipients of his inheritance, repeating his father before him—who left his entire estate to his second wife, and fifth child. The children from his first marriage were, expectedly, disinherited.

It must also be mentioned that Jeremy lost his capacity to father more children after a performed vasectomy while our third child was still in the womb. Six weeks following surgery, and the urologist declared him incapable of ever again reproducing.

Possessions and Inheritance

"I have seen another evil under the sun, and it weighs heavily on mankind: God gives some people wealth, possessions and honor, so that they lack nothing their hearts desire, but God does not grant them the ability to enjoy them, and strangers enjoy them instead"

"A man may have a hundred children and live many years; yet no matter how long he lives, he cannot enjoy his prosperity...I say that a stillborn child is better off than he. It comes without meaning, it departs in darkness, and in darkness its name is shrouded. Though it never saw the sun or knew anything, it has more rest than does that man—even if he lives a thousand years twice over but fails to enjoy his prosperity..." (Ecclesiastes 6:1-6)

"I have seen a grievous evil under the sun: wealth hoarded to the harm of its owners, or wealth lost through some misfortune, so that when they have children there is nothing left for them to inherit" (Ecclesiastes 5:13-14)

First to Fourth Generations

While growing up, Jeremy and his siblings were, for the most part, ignored by their father. Years later, and after their mother passed, they again reunited. Only then could they accept his current wife and their half-sibling, or be considered part of the man's family.

Situations in Jeremy's childhood also scarred him for life. And, for this reason, I became his punching bag. He was also second generation as referenced in the Bible.

Following our divorce he married a woman whose baby he was told was biologically his, but later learned wasn't. (A previous surgery prevented that possibility.)

Several grandchildren of my father-in-law, as third-generation, have now surrendered to infidelity and divorce as recipients of the family curse as referenced in the Bible. Time will tell if the fourth generation—the great-grandchildren—are effected by this same curse.

Most family histories will include a Back Sheep. It may be rare, or generational. And yet, some families will never conceive of such an occurrence within their own family unit. But, if members search closely, an odd one may surface.

Kyle, my husband of over twenty-four years, also raised my children as his own. However, the natural disposition of a child is to follow in their biological father's footsteps. Although complicated, this often renders good advice and Christian training from mother and step-father as null, and void.

My children, now in their thirties, have their own demons to conquer as they reap the residual damage created by those before them.

In 2004 the youngest died in a car crash at the age of twenty-two. As a teen he used drugs and alcohol to deaden his emotional controversies. He was also a special needs child—with disabilities most likely stemming from intentional stress caused by Jeremy, his biological father, while still in the womb.

However, and to whomever it concerns, the blood line stops here.

"Oh, that their hearts would be inclined to fear me and keep all my commands always, so that it might go well with them and their children forever!" (Deuteronomy 5:29)

Actions are easily justifiable if one becomes a chronic liar.

Strongholds

The hold an abusive man has over a former partner doesn't always end with divorce. There are instances when it continues for years and years. Fear, anxiety, and terror can also reign long after a relationship has ended.

It's often difficult to rid oneself of mind manipulation. The reality of truth—that he really is out of your life—may be hard to grasp as former exploitations have psychologically strangled the mind.

It may take years of time to release the emotional clutch a perpetrator's mistreatment generated during time spent together, or while married. Because your self-respect has been smothered, your motivation to enjoy life has also been choked from existence.

It may be difficult to move beyond all the strongholds that long held you captive. But be encouraged. God will be your advocate as you regain your independence as a survivor of domestic violence.

Outside scars eventually heal. Emotional pain—it lingers still

Chapter Eighteen

Death of a Marriage

Divorce, no matter the reason, can be as painful as physical death as it slices through the very core of a valued promise—vows to love, honor, and cherish until the day of natural death. Those who have suffered the effects of a dying marriage can certify there's nothing worse than a bad marriage. And those who found a loving, faithful partner can confirm there's nothing better than a good one.

But when divorce is inevitable, trust and honor are replaced with dishonor and mistrust. Hopes, desires, and plans are then dumped, recycled, or cast-off only to create a landscape of remorse, anger, and pain. These feelings are also similar to the stages of grief that follow the death of a loved one.

Divorce can also be illustrated as a demonstration of split firewood. Your very existence has been devalued, and your worth scattered as litter on the ground. This exploitation can also leave emotions as open and exposed as piles of raw sewage. A natural death is often easier to tolerate than the death of a marriage.

Residual scarring from an abusive marital demise often remains following a divorce. Recovery from the pain of rejection and victimization can be painful, and vicious.

Fears of loneliness and legitimate questions concerning the ability to survive on your own may become a looming terror. The struggle ahead may also be intimidating as regret and worry overwhelm the senses.

Anger at your former spouse is normal, but should

abate over time. A sense of gloom and despair, no matter the circumstance, is common. Still it's advisable to seek professional counseling if exceptional feelings of doom persist.

Another avenue is to share your experience with others in similar situations. Divorce care groups are springing up everywhere in churches, and other organizations. If controversy is unending after a marital split, find a meet-up that will embrace your hurt with reinforcements of understanding and assistance. There is hope through the support of others.

It will take time to work through your loss, as marriage was meant to be a lasting commitment. But as with all heartache, allow God's word to bring you comfort as you struggle through this period in your life. This stage, as expected, will eventually pass, and a brighter day should surface.

Realize you're not alone, or an unlabeled statistic, as divorce is more common in this generation than ever before. It may be hard to release your desire for a perfect marriage. However, there are times when your very existence will insist on the reversal of such an obligation.

"Therefore what God has joined together, let man not separate" (Mark 10:9)

Nuptials should carry one through the thick and thin of life. But all too often those dreams become shambles as promises in the marriage dissolve. Divorce strips plans into shreds. In the aftermath, way too many lives are destroyed by it.

All separations aren't justifiable, as divorce wasn't God's original plan for his people. But if children are involved, the emotional pain will be doubled. However, there are times when divorce is justifiable.

God did not intend for a woman to be a man's punching bag. Abuse in any form is never acceptable, and a reasonable incentive for divorcing. Infidelity is also legitimate, and a Biblical justification for divorce. Unfaithfulness creates insurmountable problems for the future, and someone will always be the grieving partner following this deception.

It isn't sinful to divorce a partner who is unfaithful (adulterous) if this is the road you choose to take. However, sharing guilt for another's sin should never be accepted. Shed that responsibility, and continue your life in peace.

"My people will live in peaceful dwelling places, in secure homes, in undisturbed places of rest" (Isaiah 32:18)

"But if the unbeliever leaves, let it be so. The brother or the sister is not bound in such circumstances; God has called us to live in peace" (2 Corinthians 7:15)

"Make every effort to live in peace with everyone and to be holy; without holiness no one will see the Lord" (Hebrews 12:14)

***

"For such people are false apostles, deceitful workers, masquerading as apostles of Christ. And no wonder, for Satan himself masquerades as an angel of light. It's not surprising, then, if his servants also masquerade as servants of righteousness" (2 Corinthians 11:13-15)

Their end will be what their actions deserve

Chapter Nineteen

Bible on Divorce

"Another thing you do: You flood the Lord's altar with tears. You weep and wail because He no longer pays attention to your offerings or accepts them with pleasure from your hands. You ask, "Why?"

It is because the LORD is acting as the witness between you and the wife of your youth, because you have broken faith with her, though she is your partner, the wife of your marriage covenant. Has not the LORD made them one? In flesh and spirit they are His. And why one? Because He was seeking godly offspring. So guard yourself in your spirit, and do not break faith with the wife of your youth.

"I hate **divorce,**" says the LORD God of Israel, "and I hate a man's covering himself with violence (himself meaning his wife also as they are considered as one) as well as with his garment," says the LORD Almighty. So guard yourself in your spirit, and do not break faith" (Malachi 2:13-16**)**

"Why then," they asked, "did Moses command that a man give his wife a certificate of **divorce** and send her away?

Jesus replied, "Moses permitted you to **divorce** your wives because your hearts were hard. But it was not this way from the beginning.

I tell you that anyone who **divorce**s his wife, except for marital unfaithfulness, and marries another woman commits adultery.

The disciples said to him, "If this is the situation between a husband and wife, it is better not to marry" (Matthew 19: 7-10)

"But if the unbeliever leaves, let him do so. A believing man or woman is not bound in such circumstances; God has called us to live in peace" (1 Corinthians 7:15)

"Now for the matters you wrote about: It is good for a man not to marry. But since there is so much immorality, each man should have his own wife and each woman her own husband. The husband should fulfill his marital duty to his wife, and likewise the wife to her husband. The wife's body does not belong to her alone but also to her husband. In the same way, the husband's body does not belong to him alone but also to his wife.

Do not deprive each other except by mutual consent and for a time, so that you may devote yourselves to prayer. Then come together again so that Satan will not tempt you because of your lack of self-control. I say this as a concession, not as a command. I wish that all men were as I am. But each man has his own gift from God; one has this gift, another has that.

Now to the unmarried and the widows I say: It is good for them to stay unmarried, as I am. But if they cannot control themselves, they should marry, for it is better to marry than to burn with passion.

To the married I give this command (not I, but the LORD): A wife must not separate from her husband. But if she does, she must remain unmarried or else be reconciled to her husband. And a husband must not **divorce** his wife.

To the rest I say this (I, not the LORD): If any brother has a wife who is not a believer and she is willing to live with him, he must not **divorce** her. And if a woman has a husband who is not a believer and he is willing to live with her, she must not **divorce** him. For the unbelieving husband has been sanctified through his wife, and the unbelieving wife has been sanctified through her believing husband. Otherwise your children would be unclean, but as it is, they are holy.

But if the unbeliever leaves, let him do so. A believing man or woman is not bound in such circumstances; God has called us to live in peace. How do you know, wife, whether you will save your husband? Or, how do you know, husband, whether you will save your wife?" (I Corinthians 7:1-16)

***

You may have been the faithful partner who rejected divorce. Or, perhaps you're the one who initiated it, and now feelings of regret are forming. But if counseling hasn't worked, and reconciliation isn't possible, moving forward may be your best strategy.

Allow God's word to be your guide, and never underestimate the fact that miracles do happen. Although it's often easier to blame others for our mistakes, forgiveness is best in any situation.

"Who can discern his errors? Forgive my hidden faults" (Psalms 19:12)

But if compromise isn't an option, don't be discouraged.

"Have I not commanded you? Be strong and courageous. Do not be terrified; do not be discouraged, for the LORD your God will be with you wherever you go" (Joshua 1:9)

Strive to keep anger and resentment from demolishing your dreams, and your future. Time doesn't heal all wounds. Realize it will take a great deal of it just to feel normal again. Your heart needs to heal from the pain of being mistreated, rejected, or replaced.

Allow yourself the time needed to completely recover from all former relationships.

Chapter Twenty

Certificate of Divorce

God allowed Moses, a great leader in Bible history, to give documents of divorce to his people, the Jews, in order to keep peace in the home. Tranquility was to be maintained at all costs.

This document provided an escape for the Jews who had issues too great to maintain harmony in the home. However, this reasoning has been ignored by modern church leadership for years, making it difficult to divorce an abusive spouse. In the past, the church was quick to discontinue membership with anyone who did. And family respect was forever lost.

"...Moses permitted a man to write a certificate of divorce and send her (his wife) away" (Mark 10:4) "It has been said, "Anyone who divorces his wife must give her a certificate of divorce" (Matthew 5:31) "Make every effort to live in peace with all men..." (Hebrews 12:14)

God hates divorce; but for reasons most have not yet realized. Divorce divides families and permanently scars, wounds, and shatters everyone involved. Peace in the home is disrupted when family units are destroyed, and emotionally uprooted. Children from divorced parents will remain emotionally disabled, or permanently damaged the rest of their lives.

"Like arrows in the hands of a warrior are children born in one's youth" (Psalms 127:4)

***

Betrayal

Every victim has a story to tell. Abuse, divorce, and dysfunctional relationships are common issues that need to be addressed in most families.

Honesty in sharing will help to alleviate many painful memories, and assist in establishing a more stable outcome for a marriage on the rocks. But, could infidelity be the greatest of all betrayals?

SCARS OF LIFE

The scars of life
Within—without
But deep within
Leaves not a doubt

To be the scar
That makes me mad
That causes grief
And makes life sad

A scratch, a burn
A cut, a scrape
Takes time to heal
Not time to make

The scars of life
Have left me broken
Have never mended
Yet are not spoken

©. J. Hannah Lloyd

**There's nothing worse than a bad marriage;
and nothing better than a good one.**

Chapter Twenty-One

When Truth Hurts

When the abuser is a father, his actions prove a serious lack of concern for his children.

Claws of Abuse

By Cindy Sproles

Who defines what abuse really is, and who saves us? Those are questions I still ask twenty-seven years past. It was a shameful thing, and not something I even realized was happening until I ended up eight months pregnant and in the hospital ER alone.

"Are you and your husband having issues?" The ER doctor pressed the stethoscope against my bulging tummy.

"What? No. My husband is a preacher. Things are fine between us."

The doctor peered across his glasses.

This was the first time I'd heard those words—even thought them. I wasn't abused. How ridiculous. I was a minister's wife. I loved my husband. It was a fall down the steps. I wasn't pushed. But, the doctor didn't believe me. My husband would never push me, or hit me. And, it was true. He never once laid a finger on me. I'd truly missed my footing on the staircase, and fallen. What never occurred to me were words from his mouth when I lay face-first down on the steps.

"I can't believe you're that clumsy."

My husband sat in his recliner across the room. He never stood, never offered to pick up our fourteen-month-old son. He just shook his head. When I regained my wits, I drove myself to the ER fifty-seven miles away—at night, along a desolate two-lane road.

Throughout the seven-year duration of our marriage, my husband never tried to hit me; but I can't count the times I wish he had. In fact, I stood toe-to-toe with him and asked, "Why don't you just hit me?" The pain would have at least stung, and died away.

However, words never die. They continue to dig into our souls, steal away our identity, and drive us into the pits of despair. His words could be brutal.

It had taken seven years for me to realize my husband, no longer a practicing minister, wasn't only an alcoholic, but one who would drink alone—downing a fifth of Vodka and a two liter of Sprite in one sitting.

I stood in the kitchen window and watched him pour and sip, and all the while dread the words that would fall from his mouth hours later. I was stupid—a mountain girl who was dumb because of her moral values; lazy, a bad mother, and a worse wife, irresponsible, unreliable and, here's the clincher—insignificant.

I'd much rather be slapped across the jaw than to hear those damming words repeated over and over again.

I had been raised in a middle class, southern home, in the church—defined by my values, and naïve. Abuse was something I'd hardly heard about, much less experienced as a child. Now, as a grown woman with two children under the age of three, my husband, a minister of the gospel, and a marriage counselor, was uttering those horrible words.

"This is abuse. Do you understand? This is abuse. And if you can wait thirty-days, I'll force him to make a decision to divorce. Otherwise, you'll die."

Abuse comes about in mélange ways. It's not all physical but much is mental. It happens to men and women, to children and teens. In fact, no one is exempt from its clutches when they're placed in the right situation. The claws of abuse begin with small things, and escalate to monsters that wail out of control; destroying anything and everything in its path. Mix that with drugs and alcohol and you'll find what can become a deadly mixture.

It's easy for those on the outside of abuse to utter the words, "Why doesn't she just leave?" That, in and of itself, is part of the bond that chains the abused. More times than not, the victim will never realize what happened. They've been torn, beaten down and told how lucky they are to have what they have because no one else would give it to them.

There is an indebtedness that tightens the grip of the abuser. There is fear, and the inability to see enough self-worth for a victim to care for herself. It's rarely as easy as, 'just walking away.'

But, I did walk away. On our seventh anniversary my husband took me out to a nice dinner, gave me a pretty shirt and a sweet card, then handed me a paper and said, "Tomorrow you need to go and sign the divorce papers." I sat, stunned. The slap to my heart was worse than being hit in the face.

I stared at the paper—words blurred with tears. I then stood, leaned close to my husband and said, "I will take my boys and go home. I will raise them as gentlemen, and in a godly fashion. I will never say a bad word about you. However, a day will come when you'll be forced to face your children man-to-man. And for you I say, 'God rest your soul.'"

I signed the papers, took my children and what little I could afford to move, and went home. The torturous words he had driven into me every day formed scars. From that I've become a stronger person because of the God I cried out to; "Lord save me. Please save us." Rarely a day passes that I don't read the saving scripture I clung to in Isaiah—"and by His wounds we are healed."

I'm blessed. God introduced me to a man who values me fully, who raised my boys with the same godly values and Christian beliefs I have. He loved us despite our wounds, and helped us heal. Our marriage has passed the twenty-four year mark, and our love is as fresh as it was the day we married.

I'm sure my story is so much less the pain and tragedy of others, but within it lays mercy and peace. The details only serve to breed bitterness, but forgiveness of those details preserves life.

And so I ask again: Who defines abuse, and who saves us from it? The answer lies in Isaiah 53. "But He was pierced for our transgressions, He was crushed for our iniquities; the punishment that brought us peace was on Him.

Who saves us? ... and by His wounds we are healed."

The Burley Bully

By Cathy Baker

"Get out of my way," the burly bully shouted while shoving his young son into the end-cap at Target. I paused to pay the clerk until I was certain he'd caught a glimpse of the righteous anger welling up within me. He had been seen, and I wanted him to know it.

The little boy regained his balance and cowered behind his mother, who looked to be as terrified as he was, if not more. If this man abuses his family in public, what must he do behind closed doors?

While pushing my buggy back into place, a woman approached me. "I know exactly how you feel," she said. Her head lowered as she sauntered slowly back to her mini-van. *Should I call the police? Did I even have the right to do so?* I didn't know, but this brief encounter with domestic abuse jolted the rosy-colored glasses clean off my head.

The incident was very unfortunate, but no coincidence. That terrified woman now has at least one person standing in the gap for her. I sense it may be an expansive gap in need of prayer warriors—especially on behalf of the burly bully.

Jesus looked at them and said, "With man this is impossible, but with God all things are possible" (Matthew 19:26)

Chapter Twenty-Two

Where Am I?

"O Lord, you have searched me and known me. You know my sitting down and my rising up; you understand my thought afar off. You comprehend my path and my lying down, and are acquainted with all my ways. For there is not a word on my tongue, but behold, O Lord, You know it altogether.

You have hedged me behind and before, and laid your hand upon me. Such knowledge is too wonderful for me; it is high, I cannot attain it.

Where can I go from your Spirit? Or where can I flee from your presence? If I ascend into heaven, you are there; **If I make my bed in hell**, behold, **you are there.** If I take the wings of the morning, and dwell in the uttermost parts of the sea, even there your hand shall lead me, and your right hand shall hold me.

If I say, "Surely the darkness shall fall on me, even the night shall be light about me; indeed, the darkness shall not hide from you. But the night shines as the day; the darkness and the light are both alike to you.

For you formed my inward parts; you covered me in my mother's womb. I will praise you, for I am fearfully and wonderfully made. Marvelous are your works, and *that* my soul knows very well. My frame was not hidden from you, when I was made in secret, and skillfully wrought in the lowest parts of the earth.

Your eyes saw my substance, being yet unformed. And in your book they all were written, the days fashioned for me, when as yet there were none of them.

How precious also are your thoughts to me, O God! How great is the sum of them! If I should count them, they would be more in number than the sand; when I awake, I am still with you.

Oh, that you would slay the wicked, O God!

Depart from me, therefore, you bloodthirsty men for they speak against you wickedly; your enemies take your name in vain. Do I not hate them, O LORD, who hate you? And do I not loathe those who rise up against you? I hate them with perfect hatred. I count them my enemies.

Search me, O God, and know my heart. Try me, and know my anxieties; and see if there is any wicked way in me, and lead me in the way everlasting" (Psalms 139:1-24) (NKJV)

Jesus overcame His obstacles, giving us hope that—with His help—we can also overcome ours.

Road to Recovery

"This calls for patient endurance on the part of the people of God who keep His commands and remain faithful to Jesus" (Revelation 14:12)

"He (Jesus) was chosen before the creation of the world, but was revealed in these last times for your sake. Through Him you believe in God, who raised Him from the dead and glorified Him, and so your faith and hope are in God" (1Peter 1:20-21)

Satan is behind every abusive action.

Just Listen

No one wants to listen
No one likes to hear
No one tries to help
Nothing left but fear

Should I run away
Or live here on my own
While struggling every day
More abuse to condone

My mind stays in a whirl—
Misery has me bound.
I thought I was lost
But God said, "You are found"

No reason left to fear
No one left to blame
This trial is but a season
There's hope in Jesus' name

©.J. Hannah Lloyd

Excluded

I was excluded
And left confused
Always ignored
Often abused

Forever rebuked
And left on my own
I was condemned
I was a pawn

Somewhat conflicted
My life disputed
I had no place
Was not included

Now all has changed
I'm not the same
I have no fear
I share no blame

All is forgiven,
Old thoughts deleted
My life—improved
I feel completed

©.J. Hannah Lloyd

God is With Me

I know that God is with me
I know He truly cares
I know He'll never leave me
I know He's always there

I know for His Spirit
Reminds me where I'm from
Assures me that I'm safe
And that I'll overcome

He brings me peace of mind
When my day falls apart
He places joy within me
And puts love in my heart

When deepest sorrow comes
That takes my sleep at night
I feel His Spirit with me.
And He whispers, "It's all right."

©.J. Hannah Lloyd

Chapter Twenty-Three

History of Divorce

Separation and divorce in early history created severe difficulties for everyone involved. Most faced serious consequences as they tried to re-define their lives. Divorce was humiliating as it brought shame to both families. The hatred was both intense and harsh, although laughable in today's society.

Divorce also created a vacuum of its own in early American history as state legislatures argued over whether it should even be allowed. Religious organizations were soon caught up in the debate as many members were also involved in their own divorces.

Over time, marital breakups created new interpretations of the Bible as churches became more flexible with divorce, and re-marriage. A strong deliberation is still ongoing, and creates many disturbances within the Christian community.

In the past, fear of the unknown, apprehension of future relationships, and financial burdens were associated with responses to the word *divorce*. All created apprehension, and were dreaded.

Following a divorce, parents often denied emotional or financial support to their divorced offspring. "You're on your own," was said as a reprimand to their newly divorced child. And, for the most part, they were. Shunning by friends and family was also acceptable, and expected.

Divorce within the church arena in the 1980's was also treated in similar ways, although, at that time, it was more accepted than in years past.

But in smaller churches, actions of separation and divorce were still shunned. Likewise, when I decided to flee my abusive marriage, both families were lacking in desired support, making it difficult to move forward without incredible, and almost unbeatable, odds. The undeniable fact that I had been a minister's wife only made matters worse.

Treated as a villain, and no longer accepted or forgiven for what were conceived lies, I became the accused. Disbelief was also rampant in both family and church, and reigned in unspoken contempt.

Disrespect and blame were then dumped in my lap; leaving me broken and desperate. The mockery of being shunned also created a challenge of survival amid an onslaught of contention pounding me from every direction. However, I wasn't the guilty party.

Jeremy's attitude toward our last baby was yet another strategy of placing blame for everything wrong in his life—the infidelity, the insincerity, and the ability to mistreat me, his wife, in violent ways. His abusive behavior was both intimidating and terrorizing. And yet, because no one believed he was abusive, I remained in a loveless marriage while caring for his children.

Even today I carry signs of the Battered Wife Syndrome.

Most abusers are labeled as *classic* as they display similar patterns of exploitation, manipulation, and mistreatment toward their victims.

Chapter Twenty-Four

More on Battered Wife Syndrome

Repeated physical and verbal assaults on a woman by the man in her life will result in serious physical and psychological damage to her. This violence tends to follow a predictable pattern that begins with verbal abuse, and then escalates to dangerous assaults and cruel violence. Most episodes follow an accusation as every outburst of violence is blamed on the wife.

Over time, the severity and frequency of the battering could result in death of the woman. The longer she remains under the batter's control, the more difficult it is to make a more permanent escape from her abuser.

A divorced woman can also be called a widow. And, God takes care of widows.

"A father to the fatherless, a defender of **widows,** is God in His holy dwelling" (Psalms 68:5)

"He defends the cause of the fatherless and the **widow**, and loves the alien, giving him food and clothing" (Deuteronomy 10:18)

But this promise is only available to those who keep the faith.

"May your fountain be blessed, and may you rejoice in the wife of your youth" (Proverbs 5:18)

***

Refuge

Whoever dwells in the shelter of the Most High will rest in the shadow of the Almighty. I will say of the LORD, "He is my refuge and my fortress, my God, in whom I trust." Surely He will save you from the fowler's snare and from the deadly pestilence. He will cover you with His feathers, and under His wings you will find refuge; His faithfulness will be your shield and rampart.

You will not fear the terror of night, nor the arrow that flies by day, nor the pestilence that stalks in the darkness, nor the plague that destroys at midday.

A thousand may fall at your side, ten thousand at your right hand, but it will not come near you. You will only observe with your eyes and see the punishment of the wicked. If you say, "The LORD is my refuge," and you make the Most High your dwelling, no harm will overtake you, no disaster will come near your tent. For He will command His angels concerning you to guard you in all your ways; they will lift you up in their hands, so that you will not strike your foot against a stone.

You will tread on the lion and the cobra; you will trample the great lion and the serpent. "Because he loves me," says the LORD, "I will rescue him; I will protect him, for he acknowledges my name. He will call on me, and I will answer him; I will be with him in trouble, I will deliver him and honor him.

With long life I will satisfy him and show him my salvation" (Psalms 91:1-15)

From There to Here

How did I get from there to here? The only instruction received from both parents concerning my future was the expectation of marriage. For them, children were only possessions with an inability to think for themselves.

Constant chastisement was on the agenda as *spare the rod and spoil the child* was an ingrained slogan earlier learned from an overly religious church.

"Punish them with the rod and save them from death" (Proverbs 23:14)

Impervious to the shifting world around them, change in society, essential for raising children in the generation they were born, was ignored. Information and knowledge was also restrained, and rejected. Modern technology and improvements were also denied as their belief in new information contributed to the sinful nature of man.

My father, a man of few words, required immediate compliance to his demands. My mother, in obedience to her husband and her own personal beliefs, then executed punishment for the slightest of infractions. Chastisement in the home was expected, and received on a daily basis.

Growing up in the sixties was a difficult period of time for some who lived on farms in rural America. My parents were both young adults during the World War II era. After they married, they waited ten years before any children were born. My mother was thirty-three and my father thirty-eight when I was born. However, and because of their poverty, clothing consisted of hand-me-downs from kind church members and distant relatives.

My father served in both Army and Navy during World War II, but returned a broken man. Physical wounds, for him, did not exist. However, mental and emotional scars surfaced throughout my childhood, and beyond. Yet he refused to talk about the war—only sharing pictures from his tours, and a few metal awards.

Shipwrecked in the frigid ocean for many hours while his Navel ship sank, was general knowledge. The remainder of his military history remains a mystery.

In 1957 he decided a public job was more than he could handle following the war. He quit his public job, and began to operate a poultry farm with just a hand full of chickens, and little knowledge. He was known around town as the "Chicken Man' but with only enough customers to eek out a meager living.

My childhood consisted of hard labor seven days a week. Every hand on the farm was needed to raise enough chickens to produce enough eggs to sell to neighbors and townspeople. Coupled with a large field of hay grown for the cow, and a small vegetable garden, our family existed mainly on eggs; cooked in every conceivable way possible. Fresh vegetables, and occasional meat from half a pig, or calf raised on the farm, finished the menu.

Indifferent and uninterested, my father rarely acknowledged my existence; and only when he needed work done. Growing up on the farm was the very epitome of hard labor, disciplinary restrictions, neglect, poverty, and imposed abuse. My childhood is often described as living with Amish parents in the Eighteenth century while growing up in the Twentieth. Our family, as expected, was only as modern as electricity, running water, and a toilet in the house.

The down side was not receiving the same acceptance, or support, an Amish family would provide for a child. Instead, I was thrust into a modern world by overly strict and religious parents who lived an out-of-date lifestyle.

My dad was not an affectionate man. Hugs and kisses were nonexistent, and words of praise never uttered. Aloof and distant, he surfaced only for work and meals. But, as a farmer's child, my help was needed for his survival. While growing up I needed his love and approval. What I didn't need, as a teenager, was a cute boyfriend. A loving father would have made a world of difference to an ignored child.

In my quest for love, flirting was essential; and brought many relationships to my doorstep. Yet I remained a virgin, saving myself for the one I would one day marry.

Your parents ruin the first half of your life, and your children ruin the second.
Clarence Darrell

Chapter Twenty-Five

Who can I Trust?

Living in the darkness of repression keeps the light of freedom restrained. But with God's help, a leap through the darkened tunnel into the light is achievable.

"The man, who hates...his wife, says the LORD, the God of Israel, does violence to the one he should protect. So be on your guard, and do not be unfaithful" (2: 16)

"I hate divorce, says the LORD, the God of Israel, because the man who divorces his wife (or causes the divorce) covers his garment with violence" (Malachi 2:16)

My trust was placed in parental training received as a child, and later, the church. To remain married was the requirement, no matter the cost. It wasn't until I read a book written by Richard Roberts titled He's the God of a Second Chance did I begin to hope a release from brutality was possible. But could I survive an impending onslaught of church and family rejection if I denounced my marriage?

"But He said to me, "My grace is sufficient for you, for my power is made perfect in weakness." Therefore I will boast all the more gladly about my weaknesses, so that Christ's power may rest on me" (2 Corinthians 12:9)

Doing without food and other essentials is better than living in a house where a husband degrades, beats, and then threatens to kill you.

Where is the Love?

If I speak in the tongues of men and of angels, but have not **love**, I am only a resounding gong or a clanging cymbal. If I have the gift of prophecy and can fathom all mysteries and all knowledge, and if I have a faith that can move mountains, but have not **love**, I am nothing. If I give all I possess to the poor and surrender my body to the flames but have not **love**, I gain nothing.

Love is patient, **love** is kind. It does not envy, it does not boast, it is not proud. It is not rude, it is not self-seeking, it is not easily angered, and it keeps no record of wrongs. **Love** does not delight in evil but rejoices with the truth. It always protects, always trusts, always hopes, always perseveres. **Love** never fails. And now these three remain: faith, hope and **love.** But the greatest of these is **love**" (1 Corinthians 13:1-7, 13)

Family History

Divorce was a rare occurrence, even in the nineteen hundreds. Most of those who divorced during that time were shunned by society, and became the topic of many sermons delivered in rural churches across the south.

Jeremy's parents also divorced when he was small. His mother then raised four children on her own, but often spoke of the stigma of an unforgiving family, and church. Her divorce was triggered by a cheating husband who lied in order to cover his actions. Although he came out smelling like a rose, she was left to carry the brunt of society's judgment. He, in turn, married his lover; but she never re-married.

Their emotional baggage then became Jeremy's; whose abusive tenancies often revealed distrust and anger. In turn he heaped his rage and animosity on my shoulders, as a young bride.

On the flip side, my parents spoke in serious terms of Biblical reasons a person should never divorce. But their belief only brought acute confusion. Was it also Biblical to accept abuse from my husband? Or, should I remain steadfast in my desire for a positive outcome beyond the marriage relationship?

Church leadership strongly advised that nothing but prayer would stop the abuse. However, their advice could easily have caused my death.

In the past, battering and molestation were ignored. If a girl told her mother she was mistreated by her husband, she was admonished to remain quiet, and never speak about it. His acts of violence were then swept under the rug, and forgotten by everyone but her.

Manipulation, violence, exploitation, foul language, indecent vulgarity, insults, cruelty, injuries, and swearing are now considered abuse.

Even in today's society, violence in the home remains a challenge. Although information is available for the abused, many women remain with their children in dangerous situations. Fear may be the reason why.

Due to a serious lack of understanding, ramifications for the abused will have serious side effects. Women and children often become permanently damaged, both physically and emotionally, if they remain in harm's way. Fear will keep many under the arm of an enraged abuser.

"No one will ever believe you," or "When you come to the door, I'll blow your brains out." These same threats were hurled at me during the course of my marriage to Jeremy. Meanwhile, and in secret, plans to escape my cleric husband were well under way.

"Husbands, love your wives and do not be harsh with them" (Colossians 3:9)

When I became an adult, my dreams of a blissful marriage were destroyed, and culminated in divorce twelve years later. Inflicted brutality was a constant threat, and systemically produced physical, mental, and emotional challenges. The scars of abuse then left a throbbing ache of residual damage long after the marriage ended.

Some memories are best left to fade away...

Chapter Twenty-Six

Rage

A victim of abuse may struggle with eating disorders, low self-esteem, or an inability to bond with others.

In later years it become obvious as to why I accepted marital battering. Beaten by my mother during childhood and long into adolescence programmed me to accept my first husband's abuse.

"Better to dwell in the wilderness, than with a contentious and angry woman" (or man) (Proverbs 21:19)

Although I loathed the abuse, I was helpless to change it. Even today I experiences self-hatred based on a former powerlessness to escape my abusers.

Deliverance from parental restraints, and later my first marriage, was enormous.

Stepping into new-found freedom then became unadulterated liberation.

God's Law vs. Man's Traditions

"...**widom** is supreme; therefore, get wisdom. Though it cost all you have, get understanding" (Proverbs 4:7)"In the past God overlooked such ignorance, but now He commands all people everywhere to repent" (Acts 17:30) "He changes times and seasons; he sets up kings and deposes them. He gives **wisdom** to the wise and knowledge to the discerning" (Proverbs 10:23) "For the LORD gives **wisdom,** and from His mouth come knowledge and understanding" (Proverbs 2:6)

"Get **wisdom,** get understanding; do not forget my words or swerve from them" (Proverbs 4:5) "Do not take revenge, my friends, but leave room for God's wrath, for it is written: "It is mine to avenge; **I will repay**," says the LORD" (Romans 12:19)

It's not about age, looks, or money. It's all about commitment.

A Blind Eye

As a young wife I easily embraced bad advice while ignoring my inner voice. And, with a blind eye, I continued to trust my parents, and the church, for guidance. However, the outcome was negative as their advice required I remain in a volatile marriage while ignoring the battering, threats of death, and physical harm that were sure to intensify if I followed their recommendation.

Twelve years later, after numerous assaults and death threats, ideas began to form in my head—plans to escape my darkened tunnel of death before Jeremy put a bullet through my head.

Over the past few years domestic violence has been exposed, and assistance is available for women all over the world who face battering on a daily basis. For me, the great escape came when I put my complete trust in God. With his help, my tunnel of despair ended at the end of a brilliant rainbow.

"Now choose life, so that you and your children may live" (Deuteronomy 30:19)

"I will restore you to health and heal your wounds, declares the LORD..." (Jeremiah 30:17)

Seek Knowledge

And he said to the human race, "The fear of the LORD—that is wisdom, and to shun evil is understanding" (Job 28:28)
"...for God did not endow with **wisdom** or give a share of good sense" (Job 39:17)"What advice have you offered to one without **wisdom**!" (Job 26:3) "The mocker **seek**s **wisdom** and finds none, but **knowledge** comes easily to the discerning" (Proverbs 14:6) "The wise store up **knowledge**, but the mouth of a fool invites ruin" (Proverbs 10:14) "Stay away from a fool, for you will not find **knowledge** on their lips" (Proverbs 14:7) "...always learning but never able to come to a **knowledge** of the truth" (2 Timothy 3:7)

Voice of Wisdom

On every path taken, ask God for wisdom so your decisions aren't flawed concerning your future. Also refuse emotions that dictate a negative outcome.

Begin all decisions with the wisdom of the Creator, and under God's covering. He alone will reveal himself in ways never expected.

But most of all, don't allow the drama of life to create your destiny. Choose wisdom, and receive favor from the LORD.

"For those who find me find life and receive favor from the Lord" (Proverbs 8:35)

"How much better to get wisdom than gold! And to get understanding is to be chosen rather than silver" (Proverbs 16:16)

***

Fear God

"The fear of the LORD is the beginning of knowledge, but fools despise wisdom and instruction. Listen, my son, to your father's instruction and do not forsake your mother's teaching. They are a garland to grace your head and a chain to adorn your neck.

My son, if sinful men entice you, do not give in to them. If they say, "Come along with us; let's lie in wait for innocent blood, let's ambush some harmless soul; let's swallow them alive, like the grave, and whole, like those who go down to the pit; we will get all sorts of valuable things and fill our houses with plunder; cast lots with us; we will all share the loot"—my son, do not go along with them, do not set foot on their paths; for their feet rush into evil, they are swift to shed blood.

How useless to spread a net where every bird can see it! These men lie in wait for their own blood; they ambush only themselves! Such are the paths of all who go after ill-gotten gain; it takes away the life of those who get it" (Proverbs 1:1-19)

It's not what happens in life, but how the situation is handled that makes us, or breaks us.

Wisdom's Rebuke

"Out in the open wisdom calls aloud, she raises her voice in the public square; on top of the wall she cries out, at the city gate she makes her speech: "How long will you who are simple love your simple ways? How long will mockers delight in mockery and fools hate knowledge?

Repent at my rebuke! Then I will pour out my thoughts to you, I will make known to you my teachings. But since you refuse to listen when I call and no one pays attention when I stretch out my hand, since you disregard all my advice and do not accept my rebuke, I in turn will laugh when disaster strikes you; I will mock when calamity overtakes you— when calamity overtakes you like a storm, when disaster sweeps over you like a whirlwind, when distress and trouble overwhelm you.

"Then they will call to me but I will not answer; they will look for me but will not find me, since they hated knowledge and did not choose to fear the LORD. Since they would not accept my advice and spurned my rebuke, they will eat the fruit of their ways and be filled with the fruit of their schemes. For the waywardness of the simple will kill them, and the complacency of fools will destroy them; but whoever listens to me will live in safety and be at ease, without fear of harm" (Proverbs 1: 20-30)

***

One can't always listen to the heart, for the heart will deceive. Instead, allow God's wisdom to be your guide. Only He can direct your path because only He knows the plans He has for you.

"Trust in the LORD with all your heart and lean not on your own understanding; in all your ways acknowledge Him, and He will make your paths straight" (Proverbs 3:5-6)

Following years of youthful mistakes, God's wisdom has proven its worth.

Seek godly wisdom, and you will travel the path of righteousness into a better life.

Without God in the equation, you're on your own.

Chapter Twenty-Seven

Divine Order

God's order in the universe established the family unit from the beginning of creation. Satan, however, works hard trying to destroy the order God created.

When a man defies God's order he will inflict abuse, cruelty, and violence on other men, women, and children. This rebellion will also cause the household to malfunction.

From the beginning of time God established the role of man, and the order of succession in the family. Man was placed as leader of the household just as God is head of the church.

"For the husband is the head of the wife as Christ is the head of the church his body, of which He is the Savior" (Ephesians 5:23)

A husband, or father, is the designated breadwinner, leader, and protector of his family; and has the greater responsibility in the family. The wife has lesser responsibility, although both have significant roles in the family unit.

Husbands, love your wives, just as Christ loved the church and gave himself up for her to make her holy, cleansing her by the washing with water through the word, and to present her to himself as a radiant church, without stain or wrinkle or any other blemish, but holy and blameless. In this same way, **husbands ought to love their wives as their own bodies.** He who loves his wife loves himself.

After all, no one ever hated his own body, but he feeds and cares for it, just as Christ does the church—for we are members of his body. "For this reason a man will leave his father and mother and be united to his wife, and the two will become one flesh." This is a profound mystery—but I am talking about Christ and the church. However, each one of you also must **love his wife as he loves himself**..." (Ephesians 5:25-32)

Man in the role of husband and father should never lead his family as dictator, ruler, or king. "The 'give me, I deserve', and 'you're my slave' mentality was never God's intention when He placed man as leader over the household. Neither did God intend that women, or children, be mistreated by the dominance of man.

He Who Would Be Chief

"He who would be chief must first be servant. "...whoever wants to become great among you must be your servant..." (Matthew 20:26)

Man must provide for his family, as well as lead.

"He must manage his own family well and see that his children obey him, and he must do so in a manner worthy of full respect. (If anyone does not know how to manage his own family, how can he take care of God's church?" (1Timothy 2:3-5)

Family First

A man's wife must come first. And, because woman was created from a rib in Adam's body, she was designed to walk beside him; not above or beneath him.

"Then the LORD God made a woman from the rib He had taken out of the man, and He brought her to the man" (Genesis 2:22).

Eve was created from a part of Adam's body which allowed her the status of walking beside him, and not beneath him. She was also fashioned to be his helper, not a servant.

"The LORD God said, "It is not good for the man to be alone. I will make a helper suitable for him" (Genesis 2:18)

When a man leads his family with the mindset he alone rules, the family is in serious danger of collapsing. But as leader of the family, he should reverence the role he was created for. "For unto whomsoever much is given, of him shall much be required:" (Luke 12:48)

A man should help his family, and be available when needed. Instead of dictating his own desires, he should love, honor, and protect his wife. He should also never dominate, or dictate what she says or does. Because Christ sacrificed for the church, man should follow His example, and willingly sacrifice for his wife, and family. "Husbands love your wives just as Christ loved the church and gave himself up for her" (Ephesians 5:25)

Sanctifying and sacrificial love are the benefits of a godly marriage. But an ungodly husband often delights in pointing out the faults and failures of his wife while refusing beneficial complements, or praise.

Most marriage vows include spoken words of promise to honor, cherish, and treasure their spouse as Christ cherishes the church.

But a man who compromises his vows believes his wife is nothing more than a possession. Her attributes are then ignored as is her role as helper, and companion. Men who systematically destroy their marriage by displaying unparalleled bitterness and anger are not walking in God's divine order.

A man should love his wife beyond her faults and shortcomings, and as a prized possession. "A wife of noble character who can find? She is worth far more than rubies. Her husband has full confidence in her and lacks nothing of value. She brings him good, not harm, all the days of her life" (Proverbs 31:10-12)

God's Gift is Family

A father should first devote time to raising his children in the fear and admonition of the Lord. This is his God-given responsibility, and not the mother's. God never intended that a mother shoulder this duty. The chief responsibility of raising children is in the father's hands.

Although both parents are accountable for their offspring, a father's role has the greater accountability. His children will follow his lead whether or not he provides spiritual leadership. He is also responsible for causing his children to turn to, or from God. Children will follow the father before they follow a mother's lead.

"Why do I have to go to church? Daddy doesn't go?"

In order to raise godly children, one must first be godly themselves. It's imperative that we take time to teach our children about God, and the plan of salvation. This responsibility lies heavily on the father.

It was difficult finding time to teach my children all they should know in the home as I was the only parent. Other women also end up in the role God intended for man. But the end result rarely turns out the way it was intended. Because, when a man rejects his role, the family is ignored, and the children are crippled—confused by the father's rejection.

When a man ignores his wife and children over a period of time, their world will crumble, and fall. He should be the one to pick them up again when they fail. By providing love and encouragement, they can regain lost ground. But by ignoring their needs and squashing their hopes he only pushes the family down again.

Try re-establishing your relationship in love, and not with a stick.

"If someone is caught in a sin, you who are spiritual should restore him gently..." (Galatians 6:1)

It's best to talk things over with an injured member, and not beat them down as a resolution. It's also best not to bond with another man just because you are lonely, or believe he will be your salvation. One must first be rescued from the abuse.

A first love should be the love of a Father.

"And, "I **will be a Father** to you, and you will be my sons and daughters, says the Lord Almighty" (2 Corinthians 6:18)

When one stumbles, restore them again in love. Man must first be a servant in order to provide guidance, love, and assistance to his family. A father is to relate to God as he relates to his own family.

Abuse and disrespect, with a lack of self-control inflicted by a husband, is one of many reasons divorce occurs. The family unit *will* break apart when a man neglects his leadership role in the way God intended.

In today's society, divorce rates continue to climb at a staggering rate. According to www.marriage101.org, the divorce rate in America is now more than fifty percent; which means one in every two marriages will break up. Divorce, however, was never God's original plan for a man and a woman.

The woman is next in leadership of the family, and provides a supportive role as wife and mother.

"Wives, submit to your husbands as to the LORD. For the husband is the head of the wife as Christ is the head of the church his body, of which he is the Savior. Now as the church submits to Christ, so also wives should submit to their husbands in everything.

Husbands, love your wives, just as Christ loved the church and gave himself up for her to make her holy, cleansing her by the washing with water through the word, and to present her to himself as a radiant church, without stain or wrinkle or any other blemish, but holy and blameless. In this same way, husbands ought to love their wives as their own bodies.

He who loves his wife loves himself. After all, no one ever hated his own body, but he feeds and cares for it, just as Christ does the church—for we are members of his body."

"For this reason a man will leave his father and

mother and be united to his wife, and the two will become one flesh. This is a profound mystery—but I am talking about Christ and the church. However, each one of you also must love his wife as he loves himself, and the wife must respect her husband" (Ephesians 5:22-33)

A wife should be able to trust her husband by submission and love. But in some cases this role places her in grave danger.

"...and he shall rule over you" (Genesis 3:16)

After twelve years of respecting Jeremy, my first husband, I realized he didn't deserve my respect. But by then it was too late as the bonds of matrimony had long been broken through assaults, abuse, verbal degradation, and infidelity. Although my father wasn't always right, he did receive my respect.

A godly man will apologize when he realizes his mistakes. But an ungodly man never acknowledges his errors, and is quick to place blame on others; more specifically the wife and children.

When I submitted to my first husband, the abuse began, and I became a battered woman. But the secret remained for years, and only because I refused to ruin Jeremy's reputation in church ministry.

God, in his mercy, covered me with compassion; although my ignorance could have cost my life. It was years before I realized the extent of His grace and mercy.

Because of church teachings, I remained silent concerning the abuse. Even when the residual of assaults became more noticeable, it could only be spoken of in undertones. Fear was the delegated factor.

God ordained the family unit. Satan, however, desires to destroy what God ordained.

Over time, the love and desire I once held for my husband died. And, by the time our marriage ended, all emotion was gone. It was killed by cruelty.

When the family unit is destroyed, the children's walk with Christ is also destroyed. However, it's the husband (and father's) place is to set the example, and demonstrate the love of Christ by action.

He is the leader, and responsible for his leadership.
Life is all about choices.

As it is with the head of the house, so it is with the family

Chapter Twenty-Eight

Family Matters

God is our example of what a father should be. Satan's plan, however, is to wipe out the family's existence. His unique deception is ripping the unit apart, bit by bit. A father is his point of entry.

According to the Bible, a husband is to be head of the household, but not dictate, rule, or dominate. Instead, he should serve, as a servant, by providing and guiding his family while relying on God for leadership.

"For unto whomsoever much is given, of him shall be much required: and to whom men have committed much, of him they will ask the more" (Luke 12:48)

How to Treat a Wife

- Love her

- Do not dominate her

- Be like Christ who is head of the church

- Sacrifice for the good of her, and the children

- Don't point out her flaws

- Cherish and treasure her as Christ treasures the church

- Praise and complement her

- Don't drag her down with indecent and degrading words

- Treat her better than you want to be treated. She is your prized possession.

- Do not hate the wife of your youth

- Don't allow bitterness and anger to destroy what was once a good relationship

The benefits of love will bring sanctification to wife and family, and comes only when the husband sacrifices his life for their sake. Children, on the other hand, will follow in their father's footsteps.

"For I have chosen him, so that he will direct his **children** and his household after him to keep the way of the LORD by doing what is right and just, so that the LORD will bring about... what He has promised him" (Genesis 18:19)

Deception and anger will lead a child away from God. But in order to raise children one will be proud of, show by example. Learn to teach in love, and not anger. Take time with your family, and your children. Don't be so busy they feel ignored.

As for the role of a woman, the words *submit* and *yield* in the Bible, misinterpreted by many in the church, literally means what it says.

"**Wives**, **submit** yourselves to your own husbands as you do to the Lord" The key point is *as you do to the Lord.*

Because submission was wrongly interpreted, I was attacked, belittled, berated, battered, and left to struggle on my own. But through experience I've learned that submission in a marriage does not mean accepting abuse. It also does not mean being subservient.

As leader in the home, the husband bares the responsibility of love by example. But many don't truly believe, or accept their authority in the way it was intended. Often it's used as an excuse to bully, and literally antagonize, threaten, and attack those placed under his protection and provision—making this scripture a stumbling block for many who abuse their authority in ways never intended by God.

"Have confidence in your leaders and submit to their **authority**, because they keep watch over you as those who must give an account. Do this so that their work will be a joy, not a burden, for that would be of no benefit to you" (Hebrews 13:17)

A husband's authority was put in place by God. But man demeans and destroys every aspect of that respect if he mistreats those he should love the most. Exactly how does God look at someone who destroys the family unit? As it goes with the head of the house, so goes the family.

"Yet He does not leave the guilty unpunished; He punishes the **children** and their **children** for the sin of the parents to the third and fourth generation" Exodus 354:7)

"The LORD is slow to anger, abounding in love and forgiving sin and rebellion. Yet He does not leave the guilty unpunished; He punishes the **children** for the sin of the parents to the third and fourth generation" (Numbers 14:18)

"Fathers, do not exasperate your **children**; instead, bring them up in the training and instruction of the Lord" (Ephesians 3:5)

"Fathers, do not embitter your **children**, or they will become discouraged" (Colossians 3:21

"Parents are not to be put to death for their **children**, nor **children** put to death for their parents; each will die for their own sin:" (Deuteronomy 24:16)

"The secret things belong to the LORD our God, but the things revealed belong to us and to our **children** forever, that we may follow all the words of this law" (Deuteronomy 29:29)

"Whoever fears the LORD has a secure fortress, and for their **children** it will be a refuge" (Proverbs 14:26)

Wrong Choices

How is it possible that a marriage beginning with love, dreams, and great intentions end up in a trash dump like a pile of rubble?

Unrealistic dreams and youthful ignorance are often the cause of disastrous decisions. Although difficult to accept, all choices *will* produce consequences. It doesn't matter how old or how young a person is—misguided decisions will result in negative conclusions. Wrong options will also cause sorrow and judgment just as good choices create reward and success.

"For God does not show favoritism" (Romans 2:11) "He causes His sun to rise on the evil and the good, and sends rain on the righteous and the unrighteous" (Matthew 5:45)

Bad choices, unrealistic dreams, and youthful ignorance are often reasons one makes wrong decisions.

Strict, religious training received as a child from my parents, and later the church, required I remain married no matter the circumstance. It was the law. Divorce was sin because the Bible said God hates it.

A television program hosted by Phil Donahue, a talk show host from years past, opened my eyes to the truth: that destruction follows a child who experiences a father inflict abuse on the mother day after day during their childhood. The crux of the show made it clear the children weren't impressed by their mother's decision to stay in the marriage. On the other hand, she believed her stay was in their best interests.

Now grown, they quickly shared their disregard for her decision. Not having an abusive father and the niceties of life would have been a better choice.

The mother left in tears.

Transformation and modification are hard to accept. People move in and out of our lives all the time, for one reason or another. And yet, love in our relationships, and freedom to exist in peace, are things that truly matter.

Friendships are most often relative to jobs or common interests, and often disappear when similarities fade. Yet, when someone close moves away, or dies, hurts surface. Life is full of twists and turns, joys and sadness. This scenario is mentioned many times in the Bible. We are no different than others in past generations. Hurt is hurt.

It may be difficult to understand why things happen the way they do. Or, we may be the one responsible, and try to blame God when our dreams dissolve. It's important, however, to realize that God is still in control. He didn't promise to remove the consequence of our bad choices. He did, however, promise to be with us during our struggles.

"Brothers, I do not consider myself yet to have taken hold of it. But one thing I do: Forgetting what is behind and straining toward what is ahead, I press on toward the goal to win the prize for which God has called me heavenward in Christ Jesus" (Philippians 3:13, 14)

Whoever loves you when you need it most should be family.

Let the Future Forget the Past

If possible, move beyond all hurt and anger created by a bad relationship. Your goal should be realistic, and also be attainable. Also be aware of those who want you to wallow in your mistakes as it makes them unaccountable for their own lack of concern.

Steps to Recovery

- Take one step at a time

- Be slow to make decisions

- Accept help when offered, but use caution.

- Don't allow others to take advantage of your situation and pull you into another pitfall. Women are resilient, and often bounce back to reality. Remember, it will take time to overcome the pain of the past.

- Learn who your true friends are

- Stay away from those who fail to understand what you've been through.

As the hare soon learned, the tortuous won the race *only* because he took his time, thought things through, and remained committed to the race.

"You will keep in perfect peace those whose minds are steadfast, because they trust in you" (Isaiah 26:3)

A Trace of Sanity

takes time. It is the last step in the healing process.

Don't beat yourself up over mistakes made. Just remember. If you have repented, there is no remembrance of the past in God's eyes.

Satan desires to kill, steal, and destroy. The domino effect may be irreversible for a man who destroys both wife and family. And, because man's faith in God has failed, his children are also affected in negative ways, and often remain in jeopardy for years to come.

"God is our refuge and strength, an ever-present help in trouble" (Psalms 46:1)

"The thief comes only to steal and kill and destroy; I have come that they may have life, and have it to the full" (John 10:10)

"Record my misery; list my tears on your scroll—are they not in your record?" (Psalms 56:8)

Bad decisions bring sorrow and judgment just as good choices bring reward and success.

Acceptance

For me, accepting the unavoidable was a tough pill to swallow. What I learned as a small child was tolerance, and carried into adulthood, and beyond.

Because the ramifications of abuse run deep, they are often traced back to childhood.

- Beatings taught pain tolerance

- Feelings didn't matter, and neither did I

- Others were right and I was wrong—acceptance of abuse without complaint

- That I lacked value

- Others were important, but I wasn't

- Being controlled taught I had no other choice
Because others made decisions for me as a child, current decisions are still difficult to make. A lack of

personal self-worth devalued my personhood, and allowed acceptance for what was not acceptable.

Anger and Bitterness

"Then your Father, who sees what is done in **secret**, will reward you" (Matthew 6:6)

"For God will bring every work into judgment, including every secret thing, whether good or evil" (Ecclesiastes 12:14)

"Therefore judge nothing before the appointed time; wait 'till the Lord comes. He will bring to light what is hidden in darkness and will expose the motives of men's hearts" (1 Corinthians 4:5)

The rapist is another example of self-indulgence. Is there ever any true remorse when one causes physical and emotional pain for a woman—even worse, a child?

There is truly no justification for a lustful soul.

"Behind your doors and your doorposts you have put your pagan symbols. Forsaking me, you uncovered your bed, you climbed into it and opened it wide; you made a pact with those whose beds you love, and you looked with **lust** on their naked bodies" (Isaiah 57:8)

"You burn with **lust** among the oaks and under every spreading tree; you sacrifice your children in the ravines and under the overhanging crags" (Isaiah 57:5)

"Do not **lust** in your heart after her beauty or let her captivate you with her eyes" (Proverbs 6:25)

Many lives are wrecked by lustful, pre-mediated arrogance. Decisions made will surely have consequences. Not only is it unfair for the victim, but families on both sides will suffer right along with them.

It's a vicious assault requiring revenge. And, who is our vindicator?

"Do not take revenge, my dear friends, but leave room for God's wrath, for it is written: "It is mine to avenge; I will repay," says the Lord" (Romans 12:19)

Women throughout history have been targets of exploitation by man. The female gender is often unable to ward off outrageous attacks from an abuser, or rapist. The psychological damage done may never heal. Even physical scars are sometimes permanent.

Many will live an isolated lifestyle following an assault. Their very existence consists of meager moments when they can briefly push aside the horror they have barely survived.

"He is driven from **light** into the realm of **darkness** and is banished from the world" (Job 18:18)

"This is the verdict: **Light** has come into the world, **but people loved darkness** instead of light **because their deeds were evil**" (John 3:19)

The process has been painfully tedious as I continue to work through the pain of the past. Yet God gently urges me forward through the murky darkness of heartache. And, slowly, I am finding my way.

A channel of confusion darkened the earlier years of my life. But when the passageway opened, I began to see a light at the end of the tunnel.

"You, LORD, are my lamp; the LORD turns my **darkness into light" (2 Samuel 22:29)**

"He reveals the deep things of **darkness** and brings utter **darkness into the light" (Job 12:22)**

Even **in darkness light** dawns for **the** upright, for those who are gracious and compassionate and righteous" (Psalms 112: 4)

Respect and protect the relationships you treasure.

Chapter Twenty-Nine

No Regrets

When I told Jeremy our third baby was on the way, he more than exploded. "Get an abortion!" he shouted. "If you don't, I'll tell everyone this baby isn't mine!"

It was difficult understanding his words because, as a minister of the gospel, he often spoke in church about the sanctity of life.

Over time, it was obvious Matthew had inherited his father's good looks, and charismatic personality. He was, without a doubt, his father's son. But Jeremy was an abusive man who detested married life. He didn't enjoy parenting his first two children, and certainly wasn't happy about the third. It was a difficult time in family history. We divorced when Matthew was three.

As a teen, Matthew struggled for identity. His father could have given him a sense of self, but didn't. Many birthdays and Christmases passed, but without recognition from his father.

As a young adult, Matthew needed serious reinforcement, and a different direction. But Jeremy wasn't interested, so he struggled alone.

He was later killed in a car crash. Could his untimely death also be the result of an absentee father?

Release the pain, forgive the oppressor, and allow all anger and hurt to slide into history

ESCAPE FROM ABUSE SURVIVAL GUIDE

Chapter Thirty

Forgiveness

Only God can repay us for all the wrongs done against us. Forgiveness doesn't necessarily mean relationship. Learn to forgive—not only the person you're at odds with, but for yourself. If we don't forgive others, how can we expect God to forgive us?

Reasons to Forgive

- Because God's word says to forgive

- Faith doesn't work if you don't forgive

- Un-forgiveness is like sludge on the inside

- It will bring inner torment

- It will interfere with having a personal relationship with God

- Because it takes away the ability to love others

- The inability to forgive will open the door to Satan if one chooses not to forgive

"Do not take revenge, my dear friends, but leave room for God's wrath, for it is written: "It is mine to avenge; I will repay," says the Lord" (Romans 12:19)

"Do not be afraid; you will not suffer shame. Do not fear disgrace; you will not be humiliated. You will forget the shame of your youth and remember no more the reproach of your widowhood (or divorce). For your Maker is your husband—the LORD Almighty is his name—the Holy One of Israel is your Redeemer..." (Isaiah 54:4, 5)

"The LORD is known by His justice; the wicked are ensnared by the work of their hands" (Psalms 9:16)

"The LORD works righteousness and justice for all the oppressed" (Psalms 103:6)

How can someone do hurtful things to a loved one, and never apologize? How can an abuser believe he's still Christian? And how can someone, as an abuser, continue serving as pastor, teacher, deacon, or member of a Christian church? Where is his conscience?

Even on their death bed some will never acknowledge the pain and suffering they inflicted on wives and children. How can one be justified if their sin is never acknowledged? And, can one be justified?

Justification comes only if sins are forgiven, and under the blood of Jesus. Some will pay for their sins while still alive. Others will reap their judgment in hell.

These are the **things** God has **revealed** to us by his Spirit. The Spirit searches **all things**, even the deep **things** of God" (I Corinthians 2:10)

Perfect love casts out all fear

Chapter Thirty-One

Running From Conflict

After lifting a handful of dirty dishes from the table, I carried them back to the kitchen, and gently placed on the counter. But, my mind was elsewhere.

"I'm tired of routine chores every day, and wasting my life away in this house," I said out loud. "I'm tired of coming home from work every evening to a sadistic husband, and being battered. I'm tired of shielding the children just to keep them safe. I need to get away. But when—and how?"

Then, after plopping down on a chair, I buried my head in my hands. "I don't want to be here anymore," I said under my breath. "This is no way to live."

People are born with survivor instincts. Yet many find it easier to run from conflict than to stand and confront. Because it took time to discover the ease of running from a challenge, it will also take time to stop running, and face the issue.

Some conflicts will resolve by themselves. But, for the record, most don't.

Negative habits and inbred family traditions often create serious problems for children in the family. Ideas long ingrained are the hardest to break away from. Abuse, negative relationships, or busy parents who ignore family issues are often repeated throughout the generations. Bad conduct, viewed through the eyes of a child, also creates fear instead of harmony.

Running from conflict is often a learned behavior.

However, nothing but time can heal negative or hurtful conduct.

Still, patterns of avoidance need to be reversed. One must learn how to confront, and resolve. But the only way to recovery is to stop the old pattern, and create a new one. It's called *confronting* instead of *running*.

- Stop running from the conflict

- Seek help from a professional

- Recognize and name the problem

- Work through conflicts instead of running away

- Manage conflicts instead of escaping from them

There are times God calms the storm. Other times He calms me

Post Traumatic Stress Disorder

Post-traumatic stress disorder is a mental health condition often triggered by a terrifying event, or a series of happenings. This particular condition releases neurological changes in the brain. Brain damage dysfunction has also been medically recorded, and is reversible with proper diagnosis, and treatment.

Also labeled as an anxiety disorder, symptoms may include flashbacks, severe apprehension, or nightmares.

Women who have suffered at the hands of an abuser will go through varying degrees of post-traumatic stress.

Painful or shocking events may cause some sufferers to have difficulty coping for a period of time. It's important, however, to take care of yourself so the events causing the syndrome can recede into history, and not return to create mental chaos that may last for months, even years. But if those events continue to shake your life up, making it impossible to manage, the diagnosis may be post-traumatic stress disorder, or PTSD as often labeled.

It's also important to seek medical treatment as soon as possible if this is the case. Ignoring the problem may encase serious long-term effects.

Symptoms of post-traumatic stress are similar to the warning signs of clinical depression. However, there are differences that need further evaluation if the problem refuses to go away.

Indications of this disorder often begin within three months following an incredibly traumatic event. But also be aware—PTSD symptoms may not appear until years following the trauma.

Re-occurring fear and rage will become explosive over time. Children and loved ones can then become the recipients of one's volatile PTSD symptoms. Suffering past events of terror often leaves a victim with sensations of extreme danger ahead, with an inability to directly control the situation.

Reactions may also be embarrassing, or cause unbelievable outcomes for the PTSD sufferer. Yet, when one feels burdensome to those around them, it's simply a cry for help. Suicide may then become the end result if not treated immediately. Although selfish in reality, the number one reason suicide occurs is a distorted impression of feeling unwanted, misunderstood, or being a burden.

Symptoms of PTSD are generally categorized as escaping, invasive memories, avoidance, increased anxiety, feeling hyperactive, or sensations of being numb.

These symptoms have been grouped into three unique categories, and listed for further evaluation.

Intrusive Memories

Disturbing memories include re-living traumatic events for minutes up to days at a time. Flashbacks may occur at unexpected moments. Nightmares, or dreams recalling the event, are powerful symptoms of this disorder, and will need treatment in order to overcome them.

Symptoms of Intrusive Memories

- Flashbacks, or re-living the trauma over and over again for days at a time

- Nightmares related to the traumatic event

- Tightening in the chest wall

- Panic over even the smallest of infractions

- Feelings of dread when confronting even the simplest situation

Avoiding the Facts

A victim will often avoid talking about, or recalling a traumatic event. Still, at times, emotional numbness may surface with just the mention of a specific, distressing event. Avoiding activities once enjoyed, or experiencing feelings of hopelessness concerning the future are also symptoms that need monitoring.

The injured party may also have trouble concentrating on any one thing, and experience difficulty maintaining close relationships.

Anxiety

A victim of PTSD will become frightened in an instant, or startled at any unexpected moment. They will also have trouble sleeping. Over time they may also become self-destructive by drinking too much, or refusing to socialize. A serious danger is isolation from others.

This disorder often carries an overwhelming sense of shame, or guilt, concerning the trauma. The victim will also see and hear things that don't exist. Most will easily become irritated, or angry. Symptoms of PTSD will also come and go at any unrelated time. But, when things in general become more stressful than normal, or reminders of a recent trauma surface, the emotional outcome may have overwhelming consequences.

It's normal to harbor negative feelings and emotions following a traumatic event. But if the aftermath ignites problems with getting things back under control, it may be time to talk with a health professional. However, if symptoms of this disorder become too severe, emergency services may be required.

Don't be afraid to ask someone for help if emotions of post-traumatic stress are too difficult to handle on your own.

Mood swings and flash backs are also considered PTSD related. Don't underestimate the relationship anxiety and stress has on any disorder. It's also not uncommon to learn a dread disease has surfaced long after an abusive relationship has ended.

Although symptoms of PTSD, anxiety, or emotional numbing come and go, most will occur when things are very stressful. Incidents may also occur that accentuate the experienced trauma. You may also hear noises that reinforce negative thoughts, or see news reports such as rape or battering, and then become overwhelmed with memories of personal assaults.

Symptoms of Avoidance or Emotional Numbing

- Feels numb emotionally

- Avoids activities once enjoyed

- Inability to remember important things

- Hears or sees things that don't exist

- Has problems sleeping

- Feels hopeless concerning the future

- Has trouble concentrating

- Struggles with emotional anxiety

- Tries to ignore recent or extended trauma

- Has difficulty overcoming guilt and shame

- Struggles with close relationships

- Maintains self-destructive actions such as drinking too much

- Is easily frightened, or startled

- Feels enraged and out of control

Medical Treatment

It's completely normal to have a wide range of feelings and emotions following any traumatic event. Fear and anxiety will surface under these circumstances. An inability to focus on everyday life, feelings of sadness, sleep deprivation, unusual eating habits, or depression exhibiting spells of crying may also occur. Nightmares or an inability to stop thinking about a recent trauma is not unusual. However, this alone does not mean a diagnosis of PTSD.

But if these events continue for more than a month or two, it's time to seek medical treatment for help in getting back on track. If diagnosed with PTSD, treatment may be necessary to stop those symptoms from controlling your life.

However, if post traumatic stress becomes severe, immediate emergency care may be needed. Call 911, contact a doctor, or have a friend or family member do it for you. The after-effects of stress can cause the victim to mentally re-live their trauma over and over again, although the situation has long passed. PTSD may also surface in unusual ways under normal circumstances.

"The LORD makes firm the steps of the one who delights in Him" (Psalms 37:23)

"You will keep in perfect peace those whose minds are steadfast, because they trust in you" (Isaiah 26:3)

"The prayer of a **righteous** person is powerful and effective" (James 5:16)

Because I've personally suffered the effects of this disorder, my perception is exceptional. Having lived through it, I now understand PTSD, and know it is survivable.

***

Panic Attacks

Panic Attack Disorder can be a serious condition if not treated properly. The ratio for persons having these attacks is one out of seventy-five. There may also be a genetic pre-disposition. If someone in your family suffers from this disorder, you may also be at risk.

Panic attacks follow an event, or series of events, that keep a person under extreme stress, and duress; often without a way to escape the pressure. Stress is the deciding factor.

A panic attack begins with a sudden surge of overwhelming fear. At that moment, panic will seize a person's ability to think in a rational way. These attacks also come without warning.

Severe panic attacks followed my divorce from Jeremy—fear that he was lurking in the shadows watching, and ready to pounce when I was least prepared.

The will of God will never send you where the grace of God will not protect you

Symptoms of Panic Attack

- Difficulty breathing

- Terrorized

- Paralyzing fear

- Racing heartbeat

- Sudden bouts of sweating

- Trembling or shaking

- Dizzy or lightheaded

- Becoming nauseous

- Cold chills, or hot flashes

- Chest pain, or racing heartbeat

- Tingling in extremities

- Feeling out of control without a remedy

- Blackouts—time lapses

Often symptoms will occur while asleep. The attack seems to come from nowhere, and causes different levels of panic to the stricken. There's no way to stop an attack from transpiring. Symptoms may pass in minutes, or last for hours. Some will re-occur at unspecified times.

The event may be fierce and lingering, although not physically dangerous. Feeling out-of-control is normal for someone who experiences panic on a regular basis. This disorder can be scary, and make one feel as if they're going crazy. It may also cause a social stigma if the attacks are witnessed by others.

There have been instances when a person under intense pressure blacks out, and is unable to recall places, things, or people she has met. Certain blocks of time can then vanish without a trace. Although seemingly awake and cognitive to others, time and events will happen that simply cannot be remembered—even later.

Time lapses are common for someone who steps beyond the premise of reality into a semi-conscious state of mind. Again, stress is the instigator of panic.

But, for some, fear of the unknown is cause enough for panic. However, if this is the case, stay away from things that cause severe stress, in order to avoid another episode. Still, if panic attacks are increasing, it may be time to seek medical treatment. A licensed therapist can provide a complete diagnosis if you are suffering from Panic Attack Disorder.

The after effects of stress may also cause a victim to mentally re-live their trauma over and over again, although the situation has long passed. Just as PTSD, panic disorder can surface in unusual ways under regular circumstances.

A person under extreme stress often acts out of frustration. Impulsive behavior can also be embarrassing and cause regret later, after the episode has ended. It's not unusual, however, for someone to fold under the pressure of an event, or excessive trauma.

Victims of abuse, spousal or other, often suffer from PTSD, and panic attacks. A person can also be apprehended with these disorders again and again, even years following the initial cause of stress. Seek medical treatment if new bouts of anxiety are overwhelming, or symptoms of either disorder surface.

Out-of-control spurts of rage, memory lapses, blocks of missing time, and delayed reaction to normal situations are all part of Panic Attack Disorder. Serious weight loss or excessive weight gain are also the after-effects of someone suffering from this disorder. Manic depressive disorder, days and weeks of utter turmoil, and moments of insane panic and fear are also normal. Even time delays for reactive response can be serious if not addressed by a practiced physician.

Many act out their aggressions on others, not realizing the consequences of their actions—or, maybe they do.

Chapter Thirty-Two

Role Reversal

To have a better understanding of both sides of gender relationship, this equation is broken down for easier evaluation.

Recover, salvage, rescue, reclaim,
and take back

Biblical Role of a Husband

"Now as the church submits to Christ, so also wives should submit to their **husbands** in everything. (Ephesians 5:24) **Husbands**, love your wives, just as Christ loved the church and gave himself up for her" (Ephesians 5:25) "In this same way, **husbands** ought to love their wives as their own bodies. He who loves his wife loves himself" (Ephesians 5:28)

"**Husbands**, love your wives and do not be harsh with them. (Colossians 3:19) Then they can urge the younger women to love their **husbands** and children (Titus 2:4) ...to be self-controlled and pure, to be busy at home, to be kind, and to be subject to their **husbands**, so that no one will malign the word of God" (Titus 2:5)

"**Husbands**, in the same way be considerate as you live with your wives, and treat them with respect as the weaker partner and as heirs with you of the gracious gift of life, so that nothing will hinder your prayers" (1 Peter 3:7)

"**Husbands,** love your wives, just as Christ loved the church and gave himself up for her" (Ephesians 5:25)

Biblical Role of a Wife

"**Wives,** in the same way submit yourselves to your own husbands so that, if any of them do not believe the word, they may be won over without words by the behavior of their wives. For this is the way the holy women of the past who put their hope in God used to adorn themselves. They submitted themselves to their own husbands" (1 Peter 3: 1-3)

"Jesus replied, "Moses permitted you to divorce your **wives** because your hearts were hard. But it was not this way from the beginning" (Matthew 19:8)

"Have nothing to do with godless myths and old **wives**' tales; rather, train yourself to be godly" (1Timothy 4:7)

The love of God removes all fear

Chapter Thirty-Three

Medical Battle

Symptoms of disease may surface during and after the devastation of serious assaults and battery. Multiple Sclerosis was mine to battle.

This disease could include weakness, extreme lack of energy, partial blindness, an excessive amount of migraines, cognitive issues, with an inability to function normally on a regular basis. Indicators are highly aggravated under extreme duress. Warning signs generated from stress accelerated by my first husband prior to our divorce then continued many years following.

When I turned thirty-nine, the secret of all unexplained symptoms was revealed. My diagnosis actually brought feelings of relief instead of fear. Learning more about the disease allowed an understanding that most, if not all, MS attacks were directly related to undeserved trauma brought on by an unstable and uncaring husband. The brutality suffered was highly problematic, and generated more stress in the home than was necessary.

Jeremy's anger would culminate into physical battering and verbal assaults, and excelled in frequency over time. These strongholds then created detrimental effects on every aspect of my life. The stresses connected with his action also became a direct re-activation of my disease.

As a child I was taught to do what I was told, and to never ask questions. What I learned carried over into adulthood. And, as an obedient wife, I obeyed my husband, believing the promises in our marriage vows were sacred, and to be honored. The end result was the necessity of escaping in order to survive.

The lingering effects of an abusive relationship will leave scars one may never completely recover from. The solution may take a short amount of time, or a lifetime to resolve; depending on the nature of the abuse, and the will of the abused.

But, there is hope for renewal. Because when we make mistakes in our relationships, God will pick up the pieces of our lives, restructure them, and orchestrate our future, if allowed.

Five Steps to Freedom

- Recovery

- Salvage

- Rescue

- Reclaim

- Take Back

"God heals the broken hearted and binds up their **wounds**" (Psalm 147:3)

Recovery from physical, emotional, or material damage following a violent relationship, or break-up, may take longer than one realizes. Broken bones, fractured minds, and the loss of cherished possessions will be difficult to accept.

Still it's imperative, as in first steps, to care for the physical as soon as possible by seeking medical attention. Wounds created from an assault, or multiple assaults, may need more attention than first realized, and in order to heal properly.

Manipulation, misuse, exploitation, insults, verbal abuse, swearing, name-calling, foul language, molestation, injury by assault, mis-use, ill-treatment, sexual abuse, and physical harm are just a few of the agonies one may have suffered at the hands of a perpetrator.

In the aftermath, don't be afraid to address the reason these injuries remain. Doctors and medical professionals need to know the truth in order to understand the entire situation, and provide everything needed to complete the healing process.

As for material goods, salvage the remnants, and be thankful for what remains. Reclaim what you can, and let go of the rest. Understand that some things may never be recoverable. Although difficult to accept, it's best to forgive the one who stole from you in order to move ahead with your life. Nothing more can be done, at this point, if the damage is beyond repair. Accept what cannot be changed, and move forward with peace in your heart.

In the future, try to immediately address anger when they surface—and they will surface from time to time. Just be aware that abusive memories may take longer to fade than physical scars.

Good Vs Evil

There was some concern for my safety on the part of my ex-in-laws, yet not enough to reach beyond the *blood is thicker than water* barrier.

But for me, escaping with my life, and the children, was all that truly mattered. Many hurtful things had to be released, and this was one of them.

God desires all creation to enjoy their life without the possibility of an untimely death. Freedom to exist in safety was only a dream as long as I remained under the same roof as my abuser.

But in order to completely recover, leave your baggage at the door, and step inside. God will meet you there.

A Loving God

God will take away your care
Have no fear
He'll meet you there

Once you step inside the lair
It's then you'll find
He's everywhere

©.J. Hannah Lloyd

Never Give up

Try to enjoy every aspect of your life, even if the after effects of violence are recent. We weren't designed for mistreatment, or rejection.

"...God, who richly provides us with everything for our enjoyment" (1Timothy 6:17)

"...that it may go well with you and that you may enjoy long life on the earth" (Ephesians 6:3)

Refuse to surrender to the pressures of others who desire you remain a frightened woman running from an abusive man. In the eyes of most, he's the one who's been done wrong.

Ignore what others see, believe in yourself, and step forward into an oasis of liberation, freedom, and independence from your oppressor. Trust in yourself to bring about the change your heart desires, and deserves.

Remember, God does heal and restore. So be strong. Be encouraged. And, be a survivor.

The companion book, *Tied to Terror-Secrets of a Battered Wife,* is a complete memoir of my abusive past, including a hazardous escape, untold hardships, and then restoration. Find out how God replaced my nightmare with peace, joy, and love; and a new husband named Kyle.

As painful as they may be, hurts from the past need to be released in order to obtain the freedom needed to move ahead with your life

Chapter Thirty-Four

The Police

A serious lack of compassion from local law enforcement allows criminal intent, violence, and assault to occur on a regular basis without dispute, or fear of arrest.

Can Small Town Police be Trusted?

Often labeled as the good old boys from locals, rural policemen repeatedly cater to their own offenders.

From North Carolina to Georgia to Tennessee, small town police have instigated negative stains over my life. Local enforcement can't always be trusted as proven by their reaction to many circumstances entrusted to them.

On three separate occasions while living in North Carolina, police were called following domestic violence episodes that left me battered, bruised, and shaken. But their refusal to engage in assistance was bewildering. After turning a deaf ear to my plight, they simply walked away. Their stance to remain neutral was stunning as a serious lack of involvement kept me stranded without resources concerning my safety, and the children's.

Life is tough, but I'm tougher.

Georgia on My Mind

A well-known insurance carrier from a small town in the state of Georgia, the town where Kyle and I moved, hired several women to man the phones for his established business. Our job was to generate lists of interested parties for salesmen to push an insurance sale. However, none were paid for time spent while in training—which turned into a fiasco.

Two weeks later, after I was hired, Mr. Shyster began to lay off his new employees, one by one. He then called my home, and told Kyle I was fired. The following day I went to work as scheduled, after deciding this coward needed to fire me in person.

Mr. Shyster was shocked when he saw me.

"I told your husband you were fired," he said. "What are you doing here?"

"You didn't tell me," I said.

"You're fired. Now get out."

After returning home, I called the Better Business Bureau to report the man. Following their instruction, I contacted the Georgia Department of Unemployment. From them I learned Mr. Shyster had broken the law by not compensating his employees for time spent while in training. He was then contacted, fined, and required to pay everyone for their time.

A few days later, as I walked through the parking lot of a local grocery store, Mr. Shyster saw me, accelerated the speed in his truck, and tried to drive me over. But when I dodged, he screeched away; leaving me frightened and shaken, and on the verge of collapse.

Still I knew better than to contact the police as some had purchased insurance from this man. And since its common knowledge local businesses befriend police departments, I realized they wouldn't believe me anyway. Instead I contacted my husband for assistance.

Kyle agreed it was best not to contact the police, but promised to take care of the assault himself.

The following day he became my knight-in-shinning-armor. Fearless and unrelenting, he confronted my aggressor at his place of business.

"Don't you ever come near my wife again," he said. "If you do I'll take you out."

Mr. Shyster, as later learned, cowered at his desk—his face covered in fear. His only comment, "That's a dangerous woman."

I never saw him again.

Tennessee Recall

Local police in another town generate yet another chronicle. Shortly after our move to Tennessee, I ventured out on a busy, four-lane highway, still under construction. But recently installed signal lights gave me pause, and I continued with caution. My driving record was immaculate, and I wanted to keep it that way.

After navigating at a snail's pace through workmen, sign holders, and concrete boulders, I stopped at the light, which was red in color, and waited for the green arrow turn signal. And when it turned green, I guided my car left as indicated.

But, in just seconds, several small-town policemen surrounded my car, lights flashing and sirens screeching, and instructed me to pull over.

A robust officer then glared at me through my now opened window. "What do you think you're doing?" he asked. His face was red, and reflected the boldness in his words.

"What did I do wrong?" Although confused, I couldn't help but ask. "I know I wasn't going too fast."

"You just ran a red light, lady," he said. "Plain as day."

I was stunned. But after noting the officer's arrogance, I decided to hold my ground. "I turned left only when the green arrow lit up."

"There's no turn signal there," he said, fingering his holster. "You ran a red light. Don't you know how dangerous that is?"

"I'm sure the turn light was green."

"Lady, you ran a red light. Let me see your license and registration."

"We just moved here," I said, and handed him the required documents. "My license hasn't yet been updated."

"You can't run red lights here," he said, and handed the license back. "But since you're a new resident, I'll only give you a verbal warning."

Meanwhile, the other officers had sauntered back to their cars, turned their flashers off, and driven away.

"Just make sure you never run another red light," he said.

Then, when I drove away, he followed a couple of miles before turning back.

After calming down, I retraced my steps. However, the route was the same. Due to road construction, the officers must have been confused. The installed lights beside the turn signal didn't function with the turn light, as is normal. However, the light with the arrow was exactly as I said it was, and turned from red to green as before.

Police ignorance is often the instigator of deception. Is it any wonder I don't trust small-town police? City cops—maybe. Small-town police—never.

And use caution. Never trust without reservation. Ask for assistance *only* from proven policemen, and protectors of the peace, who aren't the good-old-boys.

God will provide. He has—and He will.

Chapter Thirty-Five

God Is My Helper

Many moments gave serious doubt of survival following a court-ordered separation from my then husband Jeremy. During that time money was so tight every penny counted for something. But my anchor was my relationship with God. Without him on my side, hope for survival, and a better future, would never have been realized.

As a victim of domestic violence it was obvious my abuser would ultimately cause my death if I remained in harm's way. His threats could easily have been executed as my struggle was ignored by those around me. But my encouragement came from deep within. By faith I believed God would protect me, and my children, and keep us safe from harm. And, He did.

Brutal Existence

Most refuse to believe, much less admit, one of their own is an abuser. It's often easier to ignore a victim's pain than to acknowledge someone they love is a perpetrator.

"He causes His sun to rise on the evil and the good, and sends rain on the righteous and the unrighteous" (Matthew 5:45)

Jeremy had a fierce passion for preaching the gospel. He also had a dark side that manifested in cruelty to animals, as well as family. But it took years of time following our divorce to piece together the truth as it was.

When he stood before church congregations, my hope was always renewed. Still I didn't understand his compassion for others, but his lack for me, and his children. This burden, although oppressive, was shielded, and pushed deep inside; remaining only until forced into the open.

An inability to comprehend the truth kept me engaged in a mental battle of hope that he would repent, and change. But improvement never came, and I remained chained to the darkness of fear, dread, and the anticipation of another battering.

Although this chapter in my life was long, the end result was victory.

Why me?

You may ask, "Why me? Why did I make such horrible mistakes when choosing a mate?"

Realize it isn't God's fault. He gave us freedom of choice from the beginning of time to make our own decisions.

"And the LORD God commanded the man, "You are **free** to eat from any tree in the garden..." (Genesis 2:16) At this time in history, God gave us the freedom of choice.

But why did I, as a Christian, make such a huge mistake when choosing a marriage partner? And is it God's fault?

No. It is, without a doubt, directly related to ignorance and inexperience in decision-making as a young adult. Childhood restrictions from parents and the church mixed with youthful enthusiasm are to blame.

To believe a Christian doesn't make mistakes while attending church is a misnomer. I've now learned that trusting leadership can also be a mistake.

Although now subdued, religious dogma in the seventies created a strong relevance to restrictive doctrine in churches, and was believable.

Yet again, the Bible explains that God is no respecter of persons.

"For God does not show favoritism" (Romans 2:11)

"He causes His sun to rise on the evil and the good, and sends rain on the righteous and the unrighteous" (Matthew 5:45)

Realize that God's wisdom is far greater than ours.

We don't understand why we make the choices we do. Perhaps it's because we were raised without good direction as a child. Or, maybe we were too stubborn to acknowledge a bad relationship before it evolved into a more serious commitment. However, it's important to realize that God is in control even though we may have lost ours. His promise to be with us during our struggles is our only hope.

**When most memories are horrible,
the good ones are easily forgotten.**

Chapter Thirty-Six

True Wisdom

"Jesus replied, "If anyone loves me, he will obey my teaching. My Father will love him, and we will come to him and make our home with him" (John 14:23)

Because my family was poor, I instinctively knew college was out of the question. For me, setting goals was also a waste of time as they would never be unattainable. Other important elements in my childhood were also missing—guidance for achievement, and praise for accomplishment. I did, however, learn about God. And that relationship has carried me through the twists, turns, and heartaches life has thrown my way. The wisdom of this world could never teach the depth of wisdom learned at the foot of the cross.

When I realized Jesus would be with me when I died, living for Him was worth more than all the wisdom this world could provide. Instructions coated with love from God above are found on the pages of His guidebook, the Bible. His word provides all the direction one will ever need to live in perfect harmony with others.

What's most important in life is making room in our heart for Jesus. When allowed, joy and peace that passes all understanding will be ours. Then God will be with us through every trial and heartache that tries to beat us up.

True wisdom will also be ours, because Jesus cares that much for us. Living and working among people who appreciate, accept and trust is another huge step toward restoration of body, mind, and soul.

Prayer of Salvation

God desires a close relationship with everyone. If you're broken, despised, or hurting, you are a perfect candidate for his redemption.

Everyone is equal at the foot of the Cross. No matter what has happened to you, the brutality you may have accepted, or what you have done yourself—you can be forgiven.

"...for all have sinned and fall short of the glory of God" (Romans 3:23)

Acts 16:31 says, "...Believe on the Lord Jesus Christ, and you will be saved, you and your household." (NIV)

"If we confess our sins, he is faithful and just to forgive us our sins, and to cleanse us from all unrighteousness" (1 John 1:9)

I believe that Jesus Christ died, and shed His blood on a cross for my redemption. I also believe He arose again, and is now alive and well sitting at the right hand of God the Father; ready to make intercession for me.

I'm sorry for my sins, and I repent of them all. Please forgive me. Come into my heart and live in me. Save me, clean me up, and make me a child of the living God.

And now I accept him as Lord and Savior of my life.

Deliver me from the oppressor.

In the name of Jesus I pray.

| Sign name | Date of conversion |

"...I will **forgive** their wickedness and will remember their sins no more" (Hebrews 8:12)

"Jesus said, "You have now seen him (God); in fact, He is the one speaking with you" (John 9:37)

Chapter Thirty-Seven

Angel

The bed where I slept as a child was slammed hard against the wall, allowing more space in the tiny room. But during the winter it was so cold, small puffs of air would rise above my head with each tiny breath.

One night, and after my mother tucked me in bed, she climbed in beside me, and we both fell asleep. But early the next morning when I awoke, my eyes instantly rested on the wall. An angel was up against it. He smiled at me. Blonde hair framed his face, and he was dressed from head to toe in a robe of white.

Calm and fearless, I returned the smile. I knew, in an instant, this was my own guardian angel.

As a four-year-old, my knowledge of angels was limited, although I could recite the Christmas story from memory—when angels announced the birth of Jesus to the world.

Also displayed in another room was a small picture portraying two small children crossing a bridge with missing wooden planks. But that angel was dressed in colorful clothing. My angel was dressed in sparkling white.

Turning away, I glanced at my mother, who was still asleep beside me. Then I glanced back at the wall. My angel was gone.

Still I knew this angel was real. I knew what I had seen, and I knew how I felt. This was a divine appearance, and one I've never forgotten.

Angels have facilitated numerous escapes from

dangerous events in my life. What more evidence is needed than the fact of survival?

"He who dwells in the shelter of the Most High will rest in the shadow of the Almighty" (Psalms 91:1)

Utopia is a place of perfection. When battered and broken, find a place of solace—in the arms of God.

Chapter Thirty-Eight

Biblical Encouragement for the Abused

"...Whoever sows to please their flesh, from the flesh will reap destruction; whoever sows to please the Spirit, from the Spirit will reap eternal life. Let us not become weary in doing good, for at the proper time we will reap a harvest if we do not give up.

Therefore, as we have opportunity, let us do good to all people, especially to those who belong to the family of believers" (Galatians 6:7-10)

"We are hard pressed on every side, but not crushed; perplexed, but not in despair; persecuted, but not abandoned; struck down, but not destroyed" (2 Corinthians 4:8-9)

"We are therefore Christ's ambassadors, as though **God** were making his appeal through us. We implore you on Christ's behalf: Be **reconciled** to **God**" (2 Corinthians 5:20)

"For we must all appear before the judgment seat of Christ, so that each of us may receive what is due us for the things done while in the body, whether good or bad" (2 Corinthians 5:10)

"The LORD is slow to anger, abounding in love and forgiving sin and rebellion. Yet he does not leave the guilty unpunished; he punishes the children for the sin of the parents to the third and fourth generation" (Numbers 14:18)

"Oh, the depth of the riches of the wisdom and knowledge of God! How unsearchable are his judgments, and his paths beyond tracing out!" (Romans 11:33)

For the wisdom of this world is foolishness in God's sight. As it is written: "He catches the wise in their craftiness" (1 Corinthians 3:19)

"Now what I am commanding you today is not too difficult for you or beyond your reach" (Deuteronomy 30:11)

"The angel of the LORD encamps around those who fear him, and he delivers them" (Psalms 34:7)

"Fear the LORD, you his holy people, for those who fear him lack nothing" (Psalms 34:9)

"...the eyes of the LORD are on those who fear him, on those whose hope is in his unfailing love" (Psalms 33:18)

"As a father has compassion on his children, so the LORD has compassion on those who fear him" (Psalms 103:13)

"He fulfills the desires of those who fear Him; He hears their cry and saves them..." (Psalms 145:19)

"The LORD confides in those who fear him; He makes his covenant known to them" (Psalms 25:14)

"Surely the **righteous** will never be shaken; **they will be remembered forever**. They will have no fear of bad news; their hearts are steadfast, trusting in the LORD. Their hearts are secure, they will have no fear; **in the end they will look in triumph on their foes**" (Psalms 112:6-8)

"But you, LORD, are a shield around me, my glory, the One who lifts my head high" (Psalms 3:3)

"The secret things belong to the Lord our God, but the things revealed belong to us and to our children, forever..." (Deuteronomy 29:29)

"Now what I am commanding you today is not too difficult for you or beyond your reach." (Deuteronomy 30:11)

"This day I call the heavens and the earth as witnesses against you that I have set before you life and death, blessings and curses. Now choose life, so that you and your children may live" (Deuteronomy 30:19)

"...to proclaim the year of the LORD's favor and the day of vengeance of our God, to comfort all who mourn, and provide for those who grieve...to bestow on them a crown of beauty instead of ashes, the oil of joy instead of mourning, and a garment of praise instead of a spirit of despair. They will be called oaks of righteousness, a planting of the LORD for the display of his splendor" (Isaiah 61:3)

"If anyone, then, knows the good they ought to do and doesn't do it, it is sin for them" (James 4:17)

"Blessed are those who find wisdom, those who gain understanding, for she is more profitable than silver and yields better returns than gold" (Proverbs 3:13-14) (NKJV)

"You will keep in perfect peace those whose minds are steadfast, because they trust in you" (Isaiah 26:3)

"The LORD will strike ...with a plague; he will strike them and heal them. They will turn to the LORD, and he will respond to their pleas and heal them" (Isaiah 19:22)

"Even to your old age and gray hairs I am he, I am he who will sustain you. I have made you and I will carry you; I will sustain you and I will rescue you" (Isaiah 46:4)

"Do you not know? Have you not heard? The LORD is the everlasting God, the Creator of the ends of the earth. He will not grow tired or weary, and his understanding no one can fathom.

He gives strength to the weary and increases the power of the weak. Even youths grow tired and weary, and young men stumble and fall; but those who hope in the LORD will renew their strength. They will soar on wings like eagles; they will run and not grow weary, they will walk and not be faint" (Isaiah 40:28-31)

"The LORD is my rock, my fortress and my deliverer; my God is my rock, in whom I take refuge, my shield and the horn of my salvation, my stronghold" (Psalms 18:2)

"Scorn has broken my heart and has left me helpless; I looked for sympathy, but there was none, for comforters, but I found none (Psalms 69:20)

"Surely God will crush the heads of his enemies, the hairy crowns of those who go on in their sins" (Psalms 68:21)

"Blessings crown the head of the righteous, but violence overwhelms the mouth of the wicked" (Proverbs 10:6)

"Weeping may endure for a night but joy comes in the morning" (Psalms 30:5) (KJV)

Good for All

"Brothers and sisters, if someone is caught in a sin, you who live by the Spirit should restore that person gently. But watch yourselves, or you also may be tempted. Carry each other's burdens, and in this way you will fulfill the law of Christ. If anyone thinks they are something when they are not, they deceive themselves.

Each one should test their own actions. Then they can take pride in themselves alone, without comparing themselves to someone else, for each one should carry their own load. Nevertheless, the one who receives instruction in the word should share all good things with their instructor.

Do not be deceived: God cannot be mocked. A man reaps what he sows. Whoever sows to please their flesh, from the flesh will reap destruction; whoever sows to please the Spirit, from the Spirit will reap eternal life.

Let us not become weary in doing good, for at the proper time we will reap a harvest if we do not give up.

Therefore, as we have opportunity, let us do good to all people, especially to those who belong to the family of believers" (Galatians 6:1-10)

***

New Strength

"We fix our eyes not on what is seen, but on what is unseen. For what is seen is temporary, but what is unseen is eternal" (2 Corinthians 4:18)

"But the fruit of the Spirit is love, joy, peace, patience, kindness, goodness, faithfulness, gentleness, self-control" (Galatians 5:22-23)

"Now to HIM who is able to do immeasurably more than all we ask or imagine, according to His power that is at work within us, to HIM be glory in the church and in Christ Jesus throughout all generations, for ever and ever! Amen" (Ephesians 3:20-21)

"Do not be anxious about anything, but in everything, by prayer and petition, with Thanksgiving, present your requests to God. And the peace of God, which transcends all understanding, will guard your hearts and your minds in Christ Jesus" (Philippians 4:6)

"I can do all things through Christ who strengthens me" (Philippians 4:13)

"Now Faith is the assurance of things hoped for, the conviction of things not seen" (Hebrews 11:)1)

"So take a new grip with your tired hands, stand firm on your shaky legs, and mark out a straight, smooth path for your feet so that those that follow you, though weak and lame, will not fall and hurt themselves, but become strong" (Hebrews 12:12)

"...by His wounds you have been healed" (1 Peter 2:24)

"If we ask anything according to God's will, He hears us and answer...," (1 John 5:14-15)

A Warning against Hypocrisy

"Then Jesus said to the crowds and to his disciples: "The teachers of the law and the Pharisees sit in Moses' seat. So you must be careful to do everything they tell you. But do not do what they do, for they do not practice what they preach. They tie up heavy, cumbersome loads and put them on other people's shoulders, but they themselves are not willing to lift a finger to move them.

"Everything they do is done for people to see: They make their phylacteries wide and the tassels on their garments long; they love the place of honor at banquets and the most important seats in the synagogues; they love to be greeted with respect in the marketplaces and to be called 'Rabbi' by others. But you are not to be called 'Rabbi,' for you have one Teacher, and you are all brothers" (Matthew 23:1-8)

"...not lording it over those entrusted to you, but being examples to the flock" (1 Peter 5:3)

The Beatitudes

"He said: "Blessed are the poor in spirit, for theirs is the kingdom of heaven. Blessed are those who mourn, for they will be comforted. Blessed are the meek, for they will inherit the earth. Blessed are those who hunger and thirst for righteousness, for they will be filled. Blessed are the merciful, for they will be shown mercy. Blessed are the pure in heart, for they will see God. Blessed are the peacemakers, for they will be called children of God. Blessed are those who are persecuted because of righteousness, for theirs is the kingdom of heaven. "Blessed are you when people insult you, persecute you and falsely say all kinds of evil against you because of me. Rejoice and be glad, because great is your reward in heaven, for in the same way they persecuted the prophets who were before you.

"Brothers, I do not consider myself yet to have taken hold of it. But one thing I do: Forgetting what is behind and straining toward what is ahead, I press on toward the goal to win the prize for which God has called me heavenward in Christ Jesus" (Philippians 3:13, 14)

An abuser is someone once trusted who later violated that trust over and over again until nothing was left but numbness of heart.

Chapter Thirty-Nine

A New Life

I've now been married over twenty-four years to Kyle; a man who loves unconditionally, and enjoys doing things for me. I've also survived childhood abuse and neglect as well as an abusive first marriage. And, I've survived three major surgeries—one of which was directly related to the abuse suffered at the hands of my first husband. The removal of my left ovary in 1992, residual from Jeremy's final battering, was devastating; but also revealing as death had, once again, been averted.

In 1997 I was diagnosed with Multiple Sclerosis—a disease I'd battled many years without a diagnosis. An accurate conclusion for walking with a limp, staggering to the side, partial blindness, severe weakness, and other un-explained problems was a blessing; although physically and mentally challenging at times. Problems assimilating information while struggling to understand instruction are also common.

My entire life I was told I could never accomplish anything. But, over time, I chose not to believe bad instruction. By then I'd learned to trust in myself, just as I'd learned to trust in God.

During the course of our marriage, Kyle's employment transferred us to different locations. Learning different perspectives, and living in different states then allowed exposure to unique aspects of life. And yet, I'm still the same person I've always been.

But through every twist and turn on life's highway,

God has been with me. Although my recovery from abuse is still ongoing, I've learned to move beyond the deception, and into forgiveness. I've also learned to salvage what was good from the past, reclaim my health, and taken back much of what the devil had stolen.

Recovery from child abuse, and again as a battered wife, has been a challenge. There are times when I'm again a small girl struggling as a casualty of abuse. Although my parents meant well, generational ignorance is a difficult cycle to break.

Emotional wounds, bullying, and name calling from others is also significant. The blotched mindset placed on me as a small child escalated far into adulthood by way of my own ignorance, and wrongful trust. Wounds of mistreatment are also permanent reminders of just how far I had to travel in order to escape all the mental, physical, and emotional violence that once dominated my life.

My one desire was to be loved without struggling to survive. Today, Kyle and I are testimonies of love in action. For us, the past has been conquered, and the future is bright.

Where you have been hurt, others will be healed.

Nothing Hidden

"**Nothing** in all creation is **hidden** from God's sight. Everything is uncovered and laid bare **be**fore the eyes of him to whom we must give account" (Hebrews 4:13) (NIV)

"For there is **not**hing **hidden** that will **not be** disclosed, and **not**hing concealed that will **not be** known or brought out into the open" (Luke 8:17) (NIV)

"All my longings lie open **be**fore you, Lord; my sighing is **not hidden** from you" (Psalms 38:9) (NIV)

"Therefore judge nothing before the appointed time;

wait until the Lord **comes**. He will bring **to light** what is hidden in darkness and will expose the motives of the heart. At that time each will receive their praise from God" 1 Corinthians 4:5) (NIV)

"For rulers hold no **terror** for those who do right, but for those who do wrong. Do you want to be free from fear of the one in authority? Then do what is right and you will be commended" (Romans 13:3)

"Yet I am writing you a new command; its truth is seen in him and in you, because the **darkness** is passing and the **true light** is already shining" (1 John 2:8)

The past sins of an abuser *will* be revealed. Hope will then surface, and life can be fulfilling if we place our past in the hands of a loving God.

And, exactly what does this bring?

Peace and happy feet, tranquility, and the ability to sleep at night because joy comes in the morning. (Psalms 30:5)

Chapter Forty

Moving Forward

My escape from domestic violence into freedom was the most uplifting day of my life. Although shattered in body, I was exuberant in spirit. At last I was free and finally on my own.

But times were hard, both financially and physically. Often I struggled with starvation as money was tight, and food in the home only for the children.

During that time, while lacking proper nutrition, my nails began to peel, and my hair to fall out by the handfuls. Coffee, often my only nourishment, and at times dry saltines, helped to squelch the growls of hunger that caused embarrassing moments at inappropriate times.

A gripping fear of the unknown also followed my escape, and remained as persistent as did the hunger. Freedom had its drawbacks.

Although starved and thin, no longer was I a battered wife. Struggling alone, and doing without in order to obtain that freedom, has been worth more than all the tea in China.

Injustices and Forgiveness

"...forgive your brothers the sins and the wrongs they committed in treating you so badly..." (Genesis 50:17)

Reasons to Forgive

- A lack of forgiveness is like drinking poison and believing someone else will die

- The key to freedom from the past is forgiveness

- Internal offences also need to be forgiven

- Unintentional or perceived sins need to be acknowledged, and forgiven

- The essence of freedom is forgiveness

Making Decisions

- Think carefully. You may be one decision away from ruining your life.

- Don't run with fools.

- Don't run around

- Adultery is poison

- Don't run your mouth

- Don't accept foolishness over wisdom

The greatest love of all inside of you...words from a popular song by Whitney Houston taught the best love of all comes from deep within.

The Corner

Retreat from life
And calm my fears
A camouflage
Replaced by tears

When things get rough
A place to hide
My safety net
When threats collide

A spot to flee
From danger's zone
A corner patch
For me alone

Protected place
At last, secure
My corner world
The only cure

©.J. Hannah Lloyd

On Sunday-School Day

To church we all go
To learn and to grow
On Sunday school day

God's lessons we hear
We learn not to fear
On Sunday school day

Then take time for fun
To play and to run
On Sunday school day

Its days we enjoy
To each its own glory
On Sunday school day

©.J. Hannah Lloyd

Me and My Three

Resilient, strong, and free
Happy as can be
No more conformity
Just me and my three

©.J. Hannah Lloyd

Conclusion

Accepting advice from well-meaning people may be a mistake as wrong choices will be made, but for the right reasons. I was set up early on to believe that all the spiritual, physical, and mental abuse suffered my entire life was all in God's will.

From experience I now realize man's control was the driving force to this insanity. The rigidity of Christian dogma from parents, church, and others all but strangled the life out of me.

Betrayal on any level is harsh. But for me, and due to an element of secrecy, all the verbal and physical abuse I endured my entire life remained a secret for years.

In the beginning of my marriage to Jeremy, I believed he would benefit if I remained silent about the abuse. His ministry was going strong, and people had great respect for him as church pastor, and evangelist. Many were converted to Christianity under his ministry.

Yet truth has a way of exposing itself. And, once uncovered, it thunders forth, and deception is no more.

Looking back over a lifetime of injustices, heartache, disappointment, mistakes, regrets, and wrong decisions will make one re-think their objectives, and goals. It's also important to take account of ourselves, and purge our heart of un-forgiveness, animosity, bitterness—even hatred toward others.

Who can recognize our errors? Who can know our hidden thoughts?

"But blessed is the one who trusts in the Lord, whose confidence is in Him. They will be like a tree planted by the water that sends out its roots by the stream. It does not fear when heat comes; its leaves are always green. It has no worries in a year of drought and never fails to bear fruit.

The heart is deceitful above all things and beyond cure. Who can understand it? I the Lord searches the heart and examines the mind, to reward each person according to their conduct, according to what their deeds deserve" (Jeremiah 17:7-10)

***

How do I overcome all the injustices served me over a lifetime?

Forgiveness is the first step to re-thinking and re-designing our lives. Mercy for others is also essential for healing, and forgiveness.

Lastly, after we've forgiven others, we must also forgive ourselves. Only then will the weight of guilt melt into sheer freedom.

"So if the Son sets you free, you will be free indeed" (John 8:36)

And whatever effort it takes to achieve that freedom will have value beyond measure.

The End

Abbreviations

MS. Multiple Sclerosis
PTSD Post Traumatic Stress Disorder

Bibliography

Battered Wife Syndrome, information collected from www.divorcenet.com Walker, L., the Battered Woman (1979) See Walker, L., the Battered Woman Syndrome (1984) p. 95-97.

(www.Merriam-Webster.com) copyright © 2011, 2012 by Merriam-Webster, Incorporated.
All scriptures NIV unless otherwise indicated
www.biblegateway.com
__New International Version, ©2011__ (NIV) Copyright © 1973, 1978, 1984, 2011 by *Biblica* Zondervan Bible New International Version Copyright 1973, 1978, 1984 by International Bible Society® The Zondervan Corporation Grand Rapids, MI 49530 U.S.A.

Credits

Domestic Violence Resources

Domestic Violence Hotline at 1–800–799–SAFE (7233) or TTY 1–800–787–3224
Getting help for domestic violence or abuse
Where to Turn for Help

In an emergency:

Call 911 or your country's emergency service number if you need immediate assistance or have already been hurt.

Crisis Hotline: South Carolina   800-291-2139 or 800-273-5066, North Carolina 888-997-5066, Georgia 800-33 North Carolina 222-997-8128

For advice and support:

- In the U.S., call the <u>National Domestic Violence Hotline</u> at 1-800-799-7233 (SAFE).
- UK: call <u>Women's Aid</u> at 0808 2000 247.
- Canada: <u>National Domestic Violence Hotline</u> at 1-800-363-9010
- Australia: <u>National Domestic Violence Hotline</u> 1800 200 526
- Or visit <u>International Directory of Domestic Violence Agencies</u> for a worldwide list of helplines, shelters, and crisis centers.

Find a safe place to stay:

Call your state's branch of the National Coalition Against Domestic Violence or another local organization. For What if I or someone I know is in crisis? If you are thinking about harming yourself, or know someone who is, tell someone who can help immediately.

Call your doctor.

Call 911 or go to a hospital emergency room to get immediate help or ask a friend or family member to help you do these things.

Call the toll-free, 24-hour hotline of the National Suicide Prevention Lifeline at 1-800-273-TALK (1-800-273-8255); 1-800-799-4TTY (4889) to talk to a trained counselor

Safe Harbor, A safe place to start a new life ~ 24 hour crisis hotline - 800-291-2139
<u>www.safeharborsc.org</u>

North Carolina~ 888-997-9129

<u>www.thehotline.org/get-help/help-in-your-area</u>
<u>www.womenindistress.com</u>

www.thehotline.org/get-help/help-in-your-area
www.womenindistress.com

Resources

Abuse: http://www.abusesanctuary.blogspot.com/

American Psychological Association: www.apa.org
Ann Landers, Fifteen Ways to Leave your Lover, newspaper article, 1978   ?
Blood Banks of North Carolina
bloodbanker.com/banks/city.php?city=Asheville&state=NC
Book: He's the God of a Second Chance 1985 -Richard Roberts-http://oralroberts.com/about/our-history/richard-roberts/

Book: Mending the Soul, book on understanding and healing abuse by Steven R. Tracy, Professor of Theology and Ethics at Phoenix Seminary in Phoenix, Arizona www.mendingthesoulministries.org

Book: When Love Goes Wrong: What to Do When You Can't Do Anything Right—Ann Jones and Susan Schechter

Divorce: www.Divorcenet.com

Declaration of Independence:
http://www.ushistory.org/declaration/document/index.htm
Domestic abuse, Amy Bonomi, associate professor at The Ohio State University

Depression and Posttraumatic stress disorder: 1998-2011 Mayo Foundation for Medical Education and research
Division, produced by ABA Publishing as a benefit to Division members. 321 N. Clark Street, Chicago, IL 60654
Divorce support: www.aboutdivorce.com

Domestic Violence Statistics
http://domesticviolencestatistics.org/domestic-violence-statistics/

Emotional Abuse, Cathy Meyer, Certified Divorce Coach, Marriage Educator and Legal Investigator, www.about.com
Endometriosis www.Wikipedia.org the free encyclopedia
Endometriosis is a gynecological medical condition in which cells from the lining of the uterus (endometrium) appear and flourish outside the uterine cavity, most commonly on the ovaries. The uterine cavity is lined by endometrial cells, which are under the influence of female hormones. These endometrial-like cells in areas outside the uterus (endometriosis) are influenced by hormonal changes and respond in a way that is similar to the cells found inside the uterus. Symptoms often worsen with the menstrual cycle. Endometriosis is typically seen during the reproductive years; it has been estimated that endometriosis occurs in roughly 6–10% of women. Symptoms may depend on the site of active endometriosis. Its main but not universal symptom is pelvic pain in various manifestations. Endometriosis is a common finding in women with infertility.

Family Black Sheep ~The New York Times
www.nytco.com
History of Divorce:
http://www.history.com/encyclopedia.do?articleId=20769
http://www.allacademic.com//meta/p_mla_apa_research citation/2/6/8/9/2/pages268925/p268925-1.php
The Judges' Journal, published quarterly, is the magazine of the American Bar Association Judicial
MayoClinic: Learn more about depression
Multiple Sclerosis www.nationalmssociety.org
Oh Be Careful Little Hands, Christian Hymn Lyrics Online
© 2008 Carden's Design
Panic attack disorder.
011 American Psychological Association, 750 First Street NE, Washington, DC 20002-4242

Sexual Abuse www.healthyplace.com

Whitney Houston's song *The Greatest Love of All* ©1985 Arista Records, Inc.

Shailagh Clark, PhD, Accredited by the Health on the Net Foundation

Contributors:

Cathy Baker, an award-winning poet who delights in observing God at work in the nuances of life, and sharing those observations through writing, journaling, and blogging. An experienced Bible teacher, Cathy leads a Bible group in her church, as well as a community Bible study for women. She and her husband Brian live in South Carolina with their answer to the empty-nest syndrome—a pampered pooch named Rupert.

Cindy Sproles, Christian Devotions Ministries - P.O. Box 6494 - Kingsport, TN 37663, christiandevotions.us, www.iBegat.com, DevoKids.com, www.DevoFest.com, devocionescristiano.com,blogtalkradio.com/Christian-Devotions

About the Author

J. Hannah Lloyd is an author, poet, and free-lance writer who lives near Greenville, South Carolina with her husband and two demanding felines.

In 2007 she was presented two awards for her work at the Blue Ridge Mountain Christian Writer's Conference in Ridgecrest, North Carolina. As a poet and writer her articles, stories, and poetry have been published in adult and children's Christian literature as well as online. She also contributes poetry bi-monthly to Critter Magazine.

Other works have been published in Slate & Style, Shemom, Harold and Banner Press in Primary Pal: Pacific Press Publishing Association in Our Little Friend, MS Focus and MS Connection Magazines, Who's DANN?—a monthly magazine, Gospel Publishing House in LIVE; a weekly journal; the Pentecostal Evangel—an Assemblies of God publication, Heartland Boating, and the Upper Room magazine.

Visit her online at www.jhannahlloyd.com

Other Books by J. Hannah Lloyd

Tied to Terror—Secrets of a Battered Wife
Death Came Quickly
Ordinary Sayings and Southern Cliché

Proof

Made in the USA
Charleston, SC
06 August 2014